# A Basic Guide To
# WRESTLING

## An Official U.S. Olympic Committee Sports Series

D1596119

The U.S. Olympic Committee

Griffin Publishing Group
Glendale, California

### Editorial Statement

In the interest of brevity, the Editors have chosen to use the standard English form of address. Please be advised that this usage is not meant to suggest a restriction to, nor an endorsement of, any individual or group of individuals, either by age, gender, or athletic ability. The Editors certainly acknowledge that boys and girls and men and women of every age and physical condition are actively involved in sports and we encourage everyone to enjoy the sports of his or her choice.

10 9 8 7 6 5 4 3 2 1


ISBN 1-882180-77-1

**Griffin Publishing**

544 W. Colorado Street
Glendale, California 91204
Telephone: 1-818-244-1470

**U.S. Olympic Committee**

One Olympic Plaza
Colorado Springs, Colorado 80909
Telephone: 1-719-632-5551

Manufactured in the United States of America

# Acknowledgments

PUBLISHER       **Griffin Publishing Group**
  PRESIDENT       **Robert M. Howland**
  DIR. / OPERATIONS       **Robin L. Howland**
  MANAGING EDITOR       **Marjorie L. Marks**
  SERIES EDITOR       **Richard D. Burns, Ph.D.**
  WRITER       **Suzanne Ledeboer**
  BOOK DESIGN       **Mark M. Dodge**
  CONSULTING EDITOR       **Freda Yoshioka**
  PROJECT COORDINATOR       **Bryan K. Howland**

USOC       **United States Olympic Committee**
  PRESIDENT       **William J. Hybl**
  EXEC. DIRECTOR       **Richard D. Shultz**
  DEP. SEC'Y. GENERAL       **John Krimsky, Jr.**

USA WRESTLING
  PRESIDENT       **Larry Sciacchetano**
  EXECUTIVE DIRECTOR       **Jim Scherr**
  DIR. / COMMUNICATIONS       **Gary Abbott**

COVER PHOTO       **Casey B. Gibson**

PHOTOS       **USA Wrestling / Bob Dunlop**
& ILLUSTRATIONS       **Staatliche Museum of Berlin**
      **National Park Service**
      **Casey B. Gibson**
      **Dick McCoy / Thumbs Up**
      **Lloyd Ostendorf**
      **National Federation of State**
      **High School Associations**
      **The National Collegiate**
      **Athletic Association**

GRIFFIN PUBLISHING EXTENDS SPECIAL APPRECIATION TO
USA WRESTLING FOR PROVIDING THE COVER PHOTO
FEATURING KURT ANGLE.

*The United States Olympic Committee*

The U.S. Olympic Committee (USOC) is the custodian of the U.S. Olympic Movement and is dedicated to providing opportunities for American athletes of all ages.

The USOC, a streamlined organization of member organizations, is the moving force for support of sports in the United States that are on the program of the Olympic and/or Pan American Games, or those wishing to be included.

The USOC has been recognized by the International Olympic Committee since 1894 as the sole agency in the United States whose mission involves training, entering and underwriting the full expenses for the United States teams in the Olympic and Pan American Games. The USOC also supports the bid of U.S. cities to host the winter and summer Olympic Games or the winter and summer Pan American Games and, after reviewing all the candidates, votes on and may endorse one city per event as the U.S. bid city. The USOC also approves the U.S. trial sites for the Olympic and Pan American Games team selections.

*On behalf of the United States Olympic Committee,*

## Welcome to the
# Olympic Sports Series

We are extremely pleased to inaugurate the Olympic Sports Series. I feel this unique series will encourage parents, athletes of all ages and novices who are thinking about a sport for the first time, to get involved with the challenging and rewarding world of Olympic sports.

This series of paperback books covers both summer and winter sports, features Olympic history and basic sports fundamentals, and encourages family involvement. Each book includes information on how to get started in a particular sport, including equipment and clothing; rules of the game; health and fitness; basic first aid; and guidelines for spectators. Of special interest is the information on opportunities for senior citizens, volunteers and physically challenged athletes. In addition, each book is enhanced by photographs and illustrations and a complete, easy-to-understand glossary.

Because this family-oriented series neither assumes nor requires prior knowledge of a particular sport, it can be enjoyed by all age groups. Regardless of an individual's level of sports knowledge, playing experience or athletic ability, this official U.S. Olympic Committee Sports Series will encourage understanding and participation in sports and fitness.

*The purchase of these books will assist the U.S. Olympic Team. This series supports the Olympic mission and serves importantly to enhance participation in the Olympic and Pan American Games.*

*John Krimsky, Jr.*
Secretary General

# Contents

Welcome to the Olympic Sports Series .................................................. v

WRESTLING & THE OLYMPICS ................................................. 1
Wrestling's Heritage ................................................................. 1
Ancient Wrestling ..................................................................... 2
Styles ............................................................................................ 3
Pancratium ................................................................................. 3
Wrestling in the Ancient Olympic Games .............................. 4
Wrestling in the Middle Ages ................................................. 4

MODERN WRESTLING .............................................................. 7
Styles and Variations ............................................................... 7
Organizing the Sport ............................................................. 10
The Modern Olympic Games ................................................ 11
Women's Wrestling ................................................................ 28

THE 7 BASIC SKILLS ............................................................. 37
The Seven Skills ...................................................................... 37

THE MATCH ............................................................................. 49
Behind the Scenes ................................................................... 49
Equipment and Clothing ........................................................ 50
Before the Bout Begins .......................................................... 51
Officials .................................................................................... 51
The Bout and Scoring Points ................................................ 52
International Officials' Vocabulary ....................................... 55
Other International Competitions .......................................... 57

USA WRESTLING ................................................................... 61
USA Wrestling (USAW) ........................................................ 61
Divisions for Younger Wrestlers .......................................... 62

SCHOLASTIC & COLLEGIATE WRESTLING ...................... 67
Junior High & High School Wrestling .................................. 67
Collegiate Wrestling .............................................................. 72
How to Score Points ............................................................... 71
Wrestling for Fun ................................................................... 77

HEALTH & PHYSICAL FITNESS ........................................... 79
Nutrition ................................................................................... 79
Precautions .............................................................................. 83
Vision and Dental Care .......................................................... 86
Physical Fitness and Conditioning ........................................ 87

**SAFETY & FIRST AID** ............................................................... **89**
Safety First ............................................................................. 89
The First Aid Kit ..................................................................... 90
Treatment ................................................................................ 92
Breathing and Heat Problems ................................................. 96

**GUIDELINES** ............................................................................ **97**
Hints for Parents and Spectators ............................................ 97
Teams and Wrestlers ............................................................... 98
Coaches ................................................................................. 102

**WRESTLING WRAP-UP** ......................................................... **103**
The Benefits of Wrestling ..................................................... 103
Athletes with Special Needs—USABA .................................. 104
Volunteering ......................................................................... 105
Coaching ............................................................................... 106
Organizations for Coaches and Officials .............................. 106
National Wrestling Hall of Fame & Museum ....................... 107

**GLOSSARY** ............................................................................. **109**
General Terms and Definitions ............................................. 109
International Terms ............................................................... 117

## *An Athlete's Creed*

The most important thing in the Olympic Games is not to win but to take part, just as the most important thing in life is not the triumph but the struggle. The essential thing is not to have conquered but to have fought well.

These famous words, commonly referred to as the Olympic Creed, were once spoken by Baron Pierre de Coubertin, founder of the modern Olympic Games. Whatever their origin, they aptly describe the theme behind each and every Olympic competition.

# WRESTLING & THE OLYMPICS

Originally a survival skill, wrestling is probably the world's oldest competitive sport, with both an ancient and a modern history, and it continues to be a way to develop the physical skills of young people. Wrestling entered the Ancient Olympic Games at the 18th Olympiad in 708 B.C., where it remained an event for nearly five centuries. Although wrestling's modern history in the Games dates from 1896, its origin dates from early recorded time.

## Wrestling's Heritage

There is no exact date for the origin of wrestling, but many ancient civilizations have left evidence of the sport in tomb carvings and written documents. Caves in France have carvings and drawings dating from 15,000–20,000 years ago, showing wrestlers in the common positions known to the modern world. The Sumerians left similar evidence on stone slabs nearly 5,000 years ago. Mythic stories tell of Gilgamesh, a ruler and protector of ancient Sumeria, who fought a bull to save the city of Uruk and used his great strength to subdue opponents—often his enemies— who then became his friends and supporters.

Archaeological pictorial evidence unearthed from the ancient civilizations of China, Japan, Babylonia, and Greece revealed glimpses of traditional wrestling as did some Egyptian hieroglyphics dating back to 2250 B.C. The tomb of Vizier Ptahhotep shows six different wrestling holds, for example. At the temple–tomb of Beni Hasan near the Nile River in Egypt, tomb carvings depict more than 200 wrestlers, many in positions that are still practiced and used by wrestlers, revealing the bonds between ancient and modern wrestling. Students of gymnastics practiced wrestling as one in a series of body building exercises, yet wrestling retained its separate identity as a sport.

Even Greek gods wrestled. The poet Pindar described how the gods, Zeus and Kronus, wrestled for possession of the universe, and the First Olympic festival in 776 B.C. was held to commemorate Zeus' victory. Homer wrote in the *Iliad* of a wrestling match between Odysseus and Ajax—and Plato, meaning "broad shoulders," was the nickname given to the philosopher because as a young man he had won so many wrestling matches (his real name was Aristocles). In Greece, young men attended wrestling schools which were social centers and considered the place to learn battle skills.

## Ancient Wrestling

Theseus, the legendary Athenian hero and slayer of the Minotaur, is credited in Greek tradition with the invention of wrestling and the rules governing the sport. Regardless of the inventor, there is no question that wrestling was important to those ancient Greek athletes, who participated in two forms of the sport—upright and pancratium.

## Styles

### Upright

Upright wrestling was the final, deciding event of the five events in the pentathlon and was similar to modern freestyle wrestling, with no holds allowed above the waist.

### Pancratium

Pancratium was a "no–holds–barred" form with boxing, hitting, and kicking allowed. It was permissible to twist your opponent's arms and legs and strangle him, but biting and gouging (presumably of eyes) were forbidden. The match had no time limit, but ended whenever one of the wrestlers gave up and admitted defeat.

### In Asia and the Americas

When the Mongols conquered India in 1526, they brought a style of wrestling known as "loose," which has evolved into the form used in Pakistan and India today. Loose wrestling begins with the opponents separated, and they are allowed to start with any permitted legal hold they choose. The style is similar to Japan's, especially in the size of its competitors and the range and finesse of their moves.

The Chinese, by 700 B.C., also competed in loose wrestling, which they probably learned from those same Mongols who later conquered India. The Japanese recorded their first wrestling bout in 23 B.C. The winner, Sukune, is the ancient model for all Japanese wrestlers. Sumo, as the sport is known, became part of annual harvest festivals in Japan, and at one time, two brothers wrestled for the Imperial Throne. We also know that centuries before Europeans explored and inhabited the Western Hemisphere, Native Americans wrestled with enemy tribes and included wrestling for sport at festivals.

## Wrestling in the Ancient Olympic Games

Wrestling entered the Ancient Olympic Games in 708 B.C. and proved to be a huge, popular success. Although discus throwers were the most popular Olympic athletes, wrestlers were second and had their own fans. Milo of Croton, the famous wrestler of antiquity, achieved thirty-two victories, which included winning six Olympic championships in a row. When he wasn't competing, Milo was well–known for his lifestyle. He carried an ox around his shoulders, broke cords tied around his neck by tensing his neck muscles, and consumed prodigious amounts of food and drink.

## Wrestling in the Middle Ages

After the Roman conquest of the Greeks, wrestling declined from a sport into a brutal contest for some competitors, but, nevertheless, continued to spread with the Roman Empire across Europe. About 800 A.D., wrestling returned as a sporting competition when knights of the Holy Roman Empire became skilled in its forms and engaged men from other countries in bouts. In the years before printed information was widely available, medieval knights followed handwritten wrestling instructions, including sketches, to guide their training.

The British were fierce regional rivals, and their first recorded wrestling match occurred in London between wrestlers from Cornwall and Devon in the 13th century. Two rival monarchs were well–known for their wrestling ability and patronage of the sport. It is reported that Francis I, King of France, once challenged King Henry VII of England to a friendly bout, which Henry lost, to his great discomfort.

*Regional Styles*

Other countries developed wrestling as a competitive sport with their own unique regional styles. The Persian Empire—Iran, today—learned wrestling from Turkish soldiers about 800 A.D., using a style known as *koresh*. Opponents wore leather pants that were long and tight and could be gripped by their opponent. *Koresh* is a variation of the loose style and spread as the Turks began to dominate the area. Today, it is the national sport of Iran, as Sumo is in Japan.

Sumo *is* different. Opponents, whose weights may top 300 pounds, try to *throw* one another to the ground or force one another out of a 4.6 meter (15–foot) circular pit filled with sand. (It isn't necessary to "pin" your opponent in order to win.) The contests usually don't last very long, as the wrestlers, in spite of their huge size, are very quick on their feet. A sumo bout ends when one of the competitors touches the ground with any part of his body, except his feet.

In modern Japan, Sumo has millions of loyal fans— from the very young to retirees—who watch the national tournaments, called *bashos*, on prime–time TV and in person. The sport is more popular than baseball, makes the front pages of newspapers, and draws audiences the way a World Series or Super Bowl does in the United States.

British style–names came from the districts where the style began, in Devon, Cornwall, Cumberland, Westmoreland, and Lancashire. The latter region played a part in the development of freestyle wrestling. In Devon, the old rules allowed you to wear sturdy shoes and kick your opponent's shins, while in Cumberland, if you lost your starting hold, or if any part of your body touched the ground, except your feet, you lost. Wrestlers in Cornwall wore canvas jackets, but were not allowed to strangle their opponents with the jacket's collar! That was strictly forbidden.

For centuries, wrestling remained local and regional, an individual's sport with little or no organization for serious competitors. Not until the end of the nineteenthth century, and the early years of the twentieth, would wrestling achieve the recognition and acquire the organization needed to make it an international sport.

# 2

# MODERN WRESTLING

During the 18th and 19th centuries, wrestling matches were common events at circuses, fairs, and expositions, attracting large crowds of fans and those who were simply curious. Abraham Lincoln, as a young man growing up and working in New Salem, Illinois, was a well–known local wrestler famous for "thrashing" his opponents. Presidents George Washington and William Howard Taft were wrestlers of some note, with Washington reportedly taking on seven challengers in a row and defeating them all. Wrestlers came in all sizes, shapes, and weights, and their bouts were played in a variety of styles, but the most popular were Greco–Roman and freestyle.

## Styles and Variations
*Greco–Roman*

Early in the 19th Century, the French developed the modern wrestling style known as Greco–Roman based on modifications to the style used by the ancient Greeks. Unlike freestyle, a wrestler cannot use his legs to attack his opponent, and no holds are allowed below the waist. You may not trip or squeeze with your legs, or push, press, or lift. Legs are for support and lifting. Therefore, upper body strength and leverage are required to perfect this wrestling style. Greco–Roman was the only form of wrestling event in the modern Olympic Games until 1904, when freestyle was added. Since 1920, both have been contested at the Olympic Games and other national and international competitions.

Courtesy Lloyd Ostendorf
**Abraham Lincoln wrestling Jack Armstrong to a draw**

*Freestyle*
Freestyle is the descendant of the Greek's upright wrestling and the Lancashire regional style, when no holds were barred. Then, tripping was allowed and

throwing your opponent to the ground three times made you the victor.

National Park Service

A young William Howard Taft

You could use your legs to make single–leg or double–leg tackles, but a scissors lock on the neck, head, or body of your opponent was forbidden. (One major difference today is that wrestlers no longer rub themselves with oil and fine sand to get better holds!) Freestyle wrestling, with some modifications, is the style used in most parts of the world and remains the most popular form in North America. (See Chapter 4, "The Wrestling Match".)

*Folkstyles*

Besides Greco–Roman and freestyle, there are 160 folkstyle, or folklore, wrestling forms played throughout the world. The Swiss use a style of wrestling known as *schwingen* (swinging) and wear special pants with strong belts. Wrestlers begin by gripping one another's belts and can lift and trip. Iceland's *glima* style makes use of belts and is popular in Syria, while the former Soviet Union follows many different regional folkstyles, all forms of "belt and jacket" style wrestling. The United States has its own folkstyle wrestling, which is practiced in high schools and colleges.

## Organizing the Sport

Prior to 1924, styles, divisions, and rules varied at each Olympic Games. It seemed that the host nations favored the styles perfected by their own athletes; therefore, the best wrestlers were often hard to identify. Some common organization seemed desirable, so individuals concerned with the future of the sport founded the *Fédération Internationale des Luttes Associées* (FILA) in 1912. FILA became the international governing body for amateur wrestling, giving the sport rules, standards, and organized competitions. This seemed to be the turning point because thereafter, amateur wrestling and wrestling bouts increased in popularity throughout the world.

## The Modern Olympic Games

Scandinavians dominated the sport in the first half of the twentieth century, and from 1908 until 1948, wrestlers from Sweden and Finland won the medals in the Greco-Roman events at the Olympic Games. The only off-year for the Finns was 1928, when a German won in Greco-Roman; however, Finns were the overall winners. These early twentieth Century wrestling events often had no time periods, so it was not unusual for matches to last for hours. One six-hour marathon bout at Stockholm in 1912 ended with no decision for the two Finnish Greco-Roman wrestlers, an exhausting event that day for everyone. The United States dominated in freestyle wrestling competitions at the beginning of the century and has won the most medals of any nation in this style during the last 100 years.

At the London Games (1948), twenty-seven nations, with a total of 266 athletes competed. Henry Wittenberg, a New York policeman with a string of 300 undefeated bouts, won a gold, although most medals went to wrestlers from Turkey and Sweden.

Turkey lost an opportunity to repeat its 1948 win at Stockholm (1952) when its entry forms, for some unknown reason, were delayed. This mishap gave first-time Soviet competitors their opportunity, and they used it well, performing best in Greco-Roman and in the total number of medals won by their wrestlers. The 1956 Games in Melbourne saw the Soviets return and build on their 1952 victories by repeating in Greco-Roman and in the overall total of medals won in wrestling.

Rome (1960) was the perfect city for this ancient sport, dominated that year by West Germany's Wilfried Dietrich. But, it was a year for the United States wrestlers to shine and, in addition, competitors from

Eastern Bloc nations began to dominate. The Soviet Union's Alexandr Medved won three gold medals in a row—at Tokyo (1964), at Mexico City (1968), and at Munich (1972)—a first in the history of modern wrestling at the Olympic Games.

During the next eighteen years (1972–1980), Eastern Bloc nations and the Soviet Union continued to excel in all classes of wrestling, even having repeat winners, but never a three–in–a–row like Medved until 1996 when Russia's Alexander Karelin won his third straight in Greco-Roman. A victory pleasing to most fans in 1980 was that of Stilianos Migiakis of Greece—the first Greek in modern times to win a gold in Greco–Roman.

Beginning in the 1980s under Milan Ercegan of Yugoslavia, the President of FILA, "total wrestling" for international competitions was instituted. The bouts are shorter—down from nine minutes to five—and they are aggressive, not passive. Penalties may be assessed if you're a passive participant. The new thrust is risk; Olympic Games wrestling is to be active, fast, and athletic.

At Los Angeles in 1984, the United States probably had its best–ever freestyle wrestling team coached by Dan Gable, the 1972 Olympic Games gold medalist. Brothers Ed and Lou Banach and Dave and Mark Schultz each won a gold. An extra–special moment for wrestler Jeff Blatnick, who had overcome Hodgkin's disease, was his gold medal in Greco–Roman. The Soviet Bloc boycotted the 1984 Games, as the United States had done in 1980, so the head–to–head opportunity for their strong teams was lost.

The 1988 Games (Seoul) saw the USSR on top in all classes—freestyle, Greco–Roman, and overall medal winner. Four years later in Barcelona, competing as the Unified Team, the former Eastern Bloc countries repeated as wrestling champions in all classes, and the United States had a strong team, but there were challenges from newcomers—South Korea, North

Korea, and Cuba in freestyle; Norway, Turkey, Hungary, Germany, Cuba, and South Korea in the Greco–Roman events. At the Centennial Olympic Games in Atlanta, the U.S. won more medals in freestyle wrestling than any other country and had the highest overall medal total for its wrestlers.

Every year since 1930, the James E. Sullivan Memorial Trophy (named after the former president of the Amateur Athletic Union) is awarded to an American athlete whose performance, example and influence as an amateur have done the most during the year to advance the cause of sportsmanship in the United States. In 1990, two–time Olympic champion wrestler John Smith received the award; in March, 1996, the Sullivan Award went to Bruce Baumgartner, gold medal winner of the 130 kg in freestyle at the Los Angeles and Barcelona Olympic Games.

B.C. Staatliche Museum, Berlin
**Wrestlers on a fifth century vase**

## Bruce Baumgartner

Baumgartner, a scholar-athlete from Indiana State University (with a Master's Degree from Oklahoma State) is now the head wrestling coach at Edinboro University in Edinboro, Pa., He was the flag-bearer for the U.S. Olympians at the opening ceremonies in Atlanta, a well-deserved honor for this champion.

Bruce took the bronze in his freestyle weight class of 130 kg. (286 lbs.) and is only the sixth American to win medals in four Olympic Games. He earned first place at the 1986, 1993, and 1995 World Championships and won the U.S. Nationals thirteen years in a row from 1983 through 1996. Baumgartner was named 1995's Outstanding Amateur Athlete—the Sullivan Award—the second wrestler to receive this honor. (John Smith won in 1990.)

The Baumgartners have three sons—Bryan, Zachary, and Dylan. He collects stamps, gardens, fishes, and enjoys woodworking.

Thirty-six-year-old Bruce has not made a final decision on retirement. In wrestling, the custom is to take off your shoes and leave them on the mat if you plan to retire. His fans will be happy to learn that Bruce's shoes are still laced.

USA Wrestling

**Bruce Baumgartner ready for action**

## Matt Ghaffari

Matt Ghaffari was born in Teheran, Iran, and is a naturalized American citizen. He won a silver medal in the Greco-Roman heavyweight (130 kg./286 lbs.) class at Atlanta. A five-time U.S. Nationals champion, he has competed in international competitions since 1989. Ghaffari took first place at the World Cup in 1990 and 1991; then repeated in 1994 and 1995.

He is assistant wrestling coach at Cleveland State University where he graduated with a degree in business. Matt and his wife Amy have three daughters—Nicole and twins, Kimia and Mary.

During the Atlanta Games, Matt visited those who were injured during the Centennial Park bombing and brushed aside the kudos when he toured Georgia Baptist Hospital. "I'm just a wrestler," he said. To the doctors, nurses, and patients he was solid gold.

Casey B. Gibson

Matt Ghaffari (on the left)

# Jeff Blatnick

In 1984, Jeff Blatnick emerged as one of the most inspirational Olympic heroes in history. Two years after being diagnosed with Hodgkin's disease and undergoing surgery and radiation therapy, he continued his pursuit of an Olympic medal in the super heavyweight division of Greco-Roman wrestling. An overwhelming underdog when the tournament began, he upset Thomas Johansson in the final to win the gold medal, the first U.S. medal of any kind in Greco-Roman wrestling. During his sixteen-year wrestling career, Blatnick won ten national titles and various international awards. Blatnick was a member of both the 1980 and 1984 U.S. Olympic teams, and he retired from competition in 1988.

Since then, in addition to his motivational speaking engagements, Blatnick has worked as a television commentator for various networks. He has appeared as an expert analyst on NBC, ABC, ESPN, MSG Network and Prime Ticket Cable.

He serves on the Board of Directors of USA Wrestling and is involved with the President's program for Physical Fitness and Sport. For his volunteer efforts, Blatnick, a 1979 graduate of Springfield College, has received numerous honors for his volunteer efforts, including U.S.A. Wrestling's 1985 Man of the Year Award.

USA Wrestling

**Jeff Blatnick and his gold medal**

## Kurt Angle

Freestyle wrestler Kurt Angle of Pittsburgh, Pennsylvania did not attend the 1996 Academy Awards because the timing conflicted with his Olympic Games training. This twenty-seven year old aspiring actor, who also has a degree in education, went on to win a gold in the 220 lbs. division of freestyle wrestling. The same evening, U.S. wrestlers Kendall Cross (125.5 lbs. division) and Townsend Saunders (149.5 lbs. division) won gold and silver medals, respectively. Cross now is an assistant coach at Harvard University and is active in wrestling programs for young people.

USA Wrestling

**Kurt Angle (center)**

## Kendall Cross

Cross won his gold medal at Atlanta in the freestyle event for the 57 kg. (125.5 lbs.) class. During high school he was Oklahoma State Champion his junior year and was the 1989 NCAA champion his junior year at Oklahoma State University, where he received a degree in business economics. Since then Cross has won the U.S. Nationals three times—1992, 1995, and 1996.

As an assistant coach at the University of North Carolina, Kendall works with young wrestlers and conducts goal-setting programs for several school districts.

Cross surfs the internet and enjoys mountain biking, rollerblading, reading, and yoga.

USA Wrestling

**Kendall Cross receiving the gold medal**

## Townsend Saunders

Townsend Saunders, freestyle silver medal winner at Atlanta in the 68 kg. (149.5 lbs.) weight class, was U.S. National champion in 1991 and 1996 and has been on USAW's Team USA since 1991. Saunders attended Torrance High School in California, where he was state runner-up his senior year. Since receiving his degree in sociology from Arizona State University in 1991, he has worked with young people as a supervisor at a county juvenile facility and is a sales representative for Home Depot—one of the companies that participates in the Olympic Job Opportunity Program.

In what may be a first for the wrestling community, medalist Townsend Saunders is married to Tricia Saunders, the seven-time U.S. Women's National champion. They live in Phoenix, Arizona with their two children, and in his spare time, Saunders fixes cars, rides motorcycles, swims, and goes in-line skating.

USA Wrestling

**Townsend Saunders overcomes his opponent**

## Tom Brands

At the Centennial Games in Atlanta, Tom Brands won a freestyle gold in the 62 kg. (136.5 lbs.) weight class by decisively outscoring four opponents by 19-1. He has a string of wrestling medals and awards going back to high school in Sheldon, Iowa, where he was state champion in his junior year. During his sophomore, junior and senior years at the University of Iowa, he was NCAA champion. After college, he won the U.S. Nationals four years in a row (1993-1996), and the World Cup in 1994 and 1995.

Tom won a gold medal at the World Championships in 1993, as did his twin brother, Terry. This was the first time that brothers had won gold at the same competition in the same year. To cap it off, Tom and Terry were named USA Wrestling Athletes of the year in 1993.

Brands has a degree in physical education and is an assistant coach at the University of Iowa.

Casey B. Gibson

**Tom Brands floors his opponent**

## Weight/Age Classes– International Competitions

### Greco–Roman & Freestyle Events, FILA & USA Wrestling

| | |
|---|---|
| **Senior Men** (19 years & older) | 130 kg. |
| (17-18 year-olds need medical certificate) | |
| **Senior Women** (19 years & older) | 41-75 kg. |
| (16-18 year-olds need medical certificate) | |
| **FILA Junior** (ages 17-20) | 46-115 kg. |
| (16-year-olds need medical certificate) | |
| **FILA Cadet** (ages 14-16) | 39-95 kg. |

## Women's Wrestling

The Spartans of Greece trained young women in the art of wrestling, but they were not part of the ancient Olympic Games and did not have a legendary role model until the third century A.D. Zenobia, Queen of Palmyra, was a strong ruler who occupied Egypt and was well–known for her skill at the sport. Wrestling for women has a sketchy history, at best, and did not appear as a recognized sport until recently.

When women take up the sport, getting started often means that a female is the lone member of a traditional all–male team and competes against young men, so it's difficult and requires above–average determination and dedication. In spite of the obstacles, more and more pre–teen girls as young as seven or eight, to those in their early twenties, are wrestling and competing at local, regional, state, national, and international competitions. The U.S. Nationals, for example, grew from twenty entrants in its initial year to 120 for the 1995 tournament.

## Wrestling Medal Winners by Country

| Year | Freestyle | Greco-Roman | Overall |
|------|-----------|-------------|---------|
| 1896 | no event | Germany | no award |
| 1904 | USA | no event | no award |
| 1906 | no event | Austria | no award |
| 1908 | Gr. Britain | Finland | Gr. Britain |
| 1912 | no event | Finland | no award |
| 1920 | USA & Finland | Finland | Finland |
| 1924 | USA | Finland | Finland |
| 1928 | Finland | Germany | Finland |
| 1932 | USA | Sweden | Sweden |
| 1936 | USA | Sweden | Sweden |
| 1948 | Turkey | Sweden | Turkey |
| 1952 | Sweden | USSR | USSR |
| 1956 | Iran | USSR | USSR |
| 1960 | Turkey | USSR | Turkey |
| 1964 | Bulgaria | USSR | USSR |
| 1968 | Japan | USSR | USSR |
| 1972 | USSR | USSR | USSR |
| 1976 | USSR | USSR | USSR |
| 1980 | USSR | USSR | USSR |
| 1984 | USA | Romania | USA |
| 1988 | USSR | USSR | USSR |
| 1992 | Unified Team | Unified Team | Unified Team |
| 1996 | USA | Poland | USA |

No Olympic Games were held in 1916 during World War I or in 1940 and 1944 during World War II.

Women compete in freestyle wrestling, and their training is as demanding as that of men, with minor variations in dress and rules.

Women wrestlers at competitions follow the same rules as men, can earn the same points, and are prohibited from making the same illegal holds. However, the weight categories are different, and the matches are shorter. Schoolgirls and Cadets wrestle for one period of 3–minutes, with no break; Juniors and Seniors wrestle for one period of 4–minutes with no break. The age categories and weight classes, as established by FILA and USA Wrestling, are different for women's wrestling, as is the dress code.

## FILA Age Divisions and Weight Classes for Women

### Schoolgirls (13–14 years old)

1. 30 kg
2. 32 kg
3. 34 kg
4. 37 kg
5. 40 kg
6. 44 kg
7. 48 kg
8. 52 kg
9. 57 kg
10. 57-62 kg

### Cadets (14–16 years old)

1. 38 kg
2. 40 kg
3. 43 kg
4. 46 kg
5. 49 kg
6. 52 kg
7. 56 kg
8. 60 kg
9. 65 kg
10. 65-70 kg

### Juniors (17–20 years old)

1. 43 kg
2. 446 kg
3. 50 kg
4. 54 kg
5. 58 kg
6. 63 kg
7. 68 kg
8. 68-75 kg

### Seniors (16 years and older)

1. 41–46 kg
2. 51 kg
3. 56 kg
4. 62 kg
5. 68 kg
6. 68-75 kg

# USAW Age Divisions and Weight Classes for Women

| Bantam<br>(7-8 years old) | Midget<br>(9-10 years old) |
|---|---|
| 1. 40 lbs. | 1. 50 lbs. |
| 2. 45 lbs. | 2. 55 lbs. |
| 3. 50 lbs. | 3. 60 lbs. |
| 4. 55 lbs. | 4. 65 lbs. |
| 5. 60 lbs. | 5. 70 lbs. |
| 6. 65 lbs. | 6. 75 lbs. |
| 7. 70 lbs. | 7. 80 lbs. |
| 8. 75 lbs. | 8. 85 lbs. |
| 9. 75+ lbs. | 9. 90 lbs. |
| (15 lb. maximum | 10. 95 lbs. |
| difference) | 11. 100 lbs. |
| (Club and state | 12. 110 lbs. |
| levels only for Bantams) | 13. 120 lbs. |
| | 14. 130 lbs. |
| | 15. 130+ lbs. |
| | (20 lb. maximum difference) |

| Novice<br>(11-12 years old) | School Girl/Boy<br>(13-14 years old) |
|---|---|
| 1. 60 lbs. | 1. 66 lbs. |
| 2. 65 lbs. | 2. 70 lbs. |
| 3. 70 lbs. | 3. 74 lbs. |
| 4. 75 lbs. | 4. 81 lbs. |
| 5. 80 lbs. | 5. 88 lbs. |
| 6. 85 lbs. | 6. 97 lbs. |
| 7. 90 lbs. | 7. 105 lbs. |
| 8. 100 lbs. | 8. 114 lbs. |
| 9. 105 lbs. | 9. 125 lbs. |

continued

### (11-12 years old)
10. 110 lbs.
11. 115 lbs.
12. 120 lbs.
13. 130 lbs.
14. 140 lbs.
15. 150 lbs.
16. 165 lbs.
17. 165+ lbs.

(25 lb. maximum difference)

### (13-14 years old)
10. 136 lbs.
11. 136+ lbs.

(30 lb. maximum difference)

### Cadet*
### (14-16 years old)
1. 83 lbs.
2. 88 lbs.
3. 94 lbs.
4. 101 lbs.
5. 108 lbs.
6. 114 lbs.
7. 123 lbs.
8. 132 lbs.
9. 143 lbs.
10. 154 lbs.
11. 154+ lbs.

(30 lb. maximum difference)

### Junior World*
### (17-20 years old)
1. 94.75 lbs.
2. 101.25 lbs.
3. 110.00 lbs.
4. 119.00 lbs.
5. 127.75 lbs.
6. 138.75 lbs.
7. 149.75 lbs.
8. 165.25 lbs.
9. 165.25+ lbs.

(30 lb. maximum difference)

### Senior
### (16 years and older)
1. 90.25 - 101.25 lbs.
2. 112.25 lbs.
3. 123.25 lbs.
4. 136.50 lbs.
5. 149.75 lbs.
6. 165.25 lbs.

There are more and more international competitions open to women, and they have done very well at those. Since 1989, American women have competed in the Women's World Championships, but Japanese women lead the world at these games, followed by female wrestlers from Norway, France, Russia, the United States, and China. However, the Americans are catching up: Tricia Saunders of Phoenix, Arizona has won two World titles, and Shannon Williams of Ontario, California has earned four world medals.

Casey B. Gibson

**Sheri Belew-Kennedy at the 1996 U.S. Nationals**

To boost the development of women wrestlers, USA Wrestling (USAW), the official governing body for amateur wrestling in the United States, sponsored its first Junior Women's Tour du Monde in the summer of 1995. This tour is for young wrestlers who are at the top of their age group, and six traveled to Sweden to train with other young women wrestlers and compete in a mini–tournament. This was not a vacation from training! Each day, the participants swam, ran track, did gymnastics drills, ran cross country, did hill running and worked out on the mat. However, they did have time to enjoy a number of cultural events with their Scandinavian hosts.

Casey B. Gibson
**Tricia Saunders at the 1996 U.S. Nationals**

That year USAW held its first development camp for women and the enthusiastic participants worked with top coaches and athletes to improve their wrestling skills. In 1996, USA Wrestling hosted its first Cadet Women's Nationals for athletes 14–16 years old.

In addition, USAW has developed a Women's Team USA program which is the national team for women wrestlers. Top competitors to watch for are Vickie Zummo (97 lbs.), Shannon Williams (116.5 lbs.), and Tricia Saunders (103.5 lbs.), Saunders has won seven national championships already. When Tricia isn't winning championships, she works as a bacteriologist.

In less than a decade, young women wrestlers have begun to build their reputations in the sport and are proving that they can enter, compete, and win at national and international level events. With increased support from families, coaches, FILA, and USAW, their medal total is bound to go up. Perhaps at a 21st Century Olympic Games, there will be a place for women wrestlers on the program.

3

# THE 7 BASIC SKILLS

Every sport has certain "basics" that are used to build the foundation for more advanced techniques and strategies. When you begin the sport of wrestling, there are six fundamental skills to learn and practice—and one more after you've gained experience—before that important first bout. Since each skill builds on the first one, it is important to learn and practice them in order.

A T–shirt, shorts, socks, and wrestling shoes are all you need for practice, by the way. (See Chapter 4, "The Wrestling Match," for detailed descriptions of competition clothes.)

## The Seven Skills

**Stance** is the correct position needed for balance, and the first skill to learn. It is from this starting point that you will make subsequent moves to attack your opponent. Position requires balance, so your weight should be distributed equally on both feet, your head should be up, and your eyes looking straight ahead. But, there's a bit more because this sport engages your entire body. Spread your feet as wide as your shoulders with your knees bent at an angle and your hips flexed, set, and square. Roll your back slightly with your shoulders in and over your knees. Tuck

your elbows in close to your body so they are inside your knees and keep your forearms inside. With your weight slightly forward, hold your hands out in front of your hips—palms forward and your fingers up.

Position Staggered, front view

**Position square, side view**

**Motion** is the ability to move and follows from your stance or position. Moving to and from your opponent depends largely on the smooth motion of your hands, arms, legs, and feet and less on strength. In the correct stance, or position, the wrestler takes short, shuffling steps and moves laterally or in a circle. This keeps his muscles flexed and ready. The wrestler never moves backward or crosses his feet. He keeps his feet spread for balance so that he can slide smoothly against his opponent.

USA Wrestling

Motion No. 1

A good way to practice motion is by getting a partner who is your size, and, literally, putting your heads together! Get into the stance position, but with your foreheads touching. Then, move smoothly to the right and left, while maintaining position.

**Changing levels** is one of the difficult basic skills because the wrestler has to use it to respond to his opponent's body moves and then react by changing his own body moves. So, be patient with yourself on this one. To change levels, start with your knees bent and your back straight. Don't bend at the waist, but think of your hips as an elevator that moves up and down vertically. Keep your head up—don't bob or nod—and try to stay on the same level as your opponent. Remember, he has learned these same basic skills, too, and can be your mirror.

USA Wrestling

**Level Change No. 1**

**Penetration** is one of the most important skills, and combined with the first three basics, it teaches you how to break your opponent's position. (Remember, that your opponent is trying to do the same thing to you.) Keep your hands moving and try to get them inside your opponent's hands. This is inside control and a definite advantage because it often allows you to break the position of your opponent by doing one of three things: If your opponent's hands are too high, with inside control, you can push your opponent's wrists up by forming a yoke between the thumb and forefinger of your hand. Or, if your opponent's hands are too low, you can slap his hands down and force him to break his position. Finally, from your inside control position, use one forearm—keep your elbows tucked in—and push his hands apart. These three methods take your opponent out of his position and allow you to penetrate.

USA Wrestling

**Level change No. 2**

Changing your level (basic skill number three]) is another way to get your opponent to break position.

Bend at the knees, lower your body and take a half step in with the foot you are driving off of. Then, penetrate by taking a deep step inside your opponent's front foot. Or, bend at the knees, lower your body and take a half step in with your back foot. Then, penetrate and drive forward and into your opponent with your other foot. Good penetration skill depends on good position, so a reminder from the lesson on stance: Keep your shoulders straight, your head up, your hips forward, and your feet straight. For smooth penetration, step, don't reach.

**USA Wrestling**

Penetration No. 2

The **Lift**, skill number five, is one of the most important basic skills. To perform a lift properly, the wrestler needs the first four skills. Remember, you are building a foundation. You need to have strength to perform lifts, of course, but equally important is the position of your hips and the hips of your opponent. Legs are the key to successful lifts, for they do the work, not your back.

**USA Wrestling**

**Lift No. 1**

To begin a successful lift, kneel on one leg and have the other bent at the knee to make a 90 degree angle.

USA Wrestling

**Lift No. 2**

Lean into your standing opponent, with your head
next to his torso. Then, wrap your arms around your
opponent's thighs and squeeze. That secures him with
your arms, which are not involved anymore, other
than in the lifting process. Keep your head straight
and under your opponent's arm. (His elbow will be

just behind your ear.) Keep your back straight and vertical and your hips lower than his.

**Backstep No. 3**

Then, use the power of your legs to complete the lift.

One way to build strength in your legs is to practice doing squats with a partner on your shoulders. Five squats are enough to start with and then switch positions with your partner. Do one or two squats if that's what's comfortable for you in the beginning, and as with any conditioning or strength–building exercise, don't overdo.

A **back step** enables you to get into position so you can lift your opponent. This skill requires rotating your hips into and under your opponent so he ends up behind you and over your hips. Keep your feet close together so your support point is small. Once you're in position, do a level change, then rotate your hips "to and through" your opponent.

With practice, you will develop "muscle memory"and should be able to perform the seven basic skills almost without thinking.

USA Wrestling

Back arch No. 1

The **back arch** is the move used to perform the incredible lifts and throws seen at the higher levels of wrestling. Therefore, it is not a skill you will learn until you've had a lot of practice and experience with the first six skills! Let your coach decide when you are ready for the back arch.

**4**

# THE MATCH

Wrestling is a year–round, indoor sport that doesn't depend on the weather, nor does it require a substantial investment in uniforms or accessories, which makes it one of the more affordable sports for a family. By now you've learned the basics and have probably had some experience wrestling at school or with a wrestling club, but haven't competed in a match where your opponents may be perfect strangers. Here is what to expect:

## Behind the Scenes

Every successful wrestling competition needs several people working behind the scenes to ensure that the competition runs smoothly. On the local level, volunteers—moms, dads, brothers, sisters, and other friends—handle many of the arrangements for setting up a competition, so wrestling can be a family and community event. At the higher levels of competition, i.e., National, World, and Olympic Games competitions, highly trained and certified FILA and USAW officials are in charge.

The following summary is based on the rules and regulations of FILA and/or USA Wrestling, the two official governing bodies for amateur wrestling taking place outside secondary and collegiate schools. (See

Chapter 6, "Scholastic and Collegiate Wrestling," for differences in equipment, clothing, mats, and scoring.)

## Equipment and Clothing

Wrestling action takes place on a mat that is 9 meters in diameter, with a border 1.20–1.50 meters wide. A red, 1–meter wide band is drawn inside the 9–meter circle and runs around the circumference. In the United States, mats used for high school and college competitions are generally used for local events.

There are some accessories used by officials, but the wrestlers need only a mat and simple gear—two singlets, shoes, and socks, and—if preferred—headgear.

A one–piece **singlet** in a stretchy, body–conforming fabric, cut low in front and back, from the chest to the hips, allows easy body movement of the arms and shoulders. For competitions, you'll need two of these—one red and one blue. Singlets are available in different lengths, so check with your coaches for the style you'll need.

**Shoes** should be made from a lightweight, soft, flexible fabric, with high tops, good ankle support, and soles designed to grip the mat. A shoe made from a combination of leather and nylon mesh is popular. Wear cotton **socks** for their comfort and ability to absorb perspiration.

The use of shoes with heels or nailed soles, shoes with buckles or with any metallic parts is prohibited. The metal or rigid tips of shoe laces must be cut off, and when you are not on the mat, remove your shoes.

Basic **headgear,** which is recommended for young wrestlers in scholastic competition, is made from lightweight plastic, fits over the head with a strap, or straps, between the ear protectors, and uses an adjustable strap that is secured across or under the chin. Headgear protects the ears from injury.

Lightweight **knee pads** may be worn, but they are not required. No jewelry may be worn or any metallic or hard objects. Besides these basic clothing requirements and prohibitions for men and women, there are variations for women wrestlers:

A T–shirt under a man's wrestling singlet is not allowed. Wear a bra without metal fittings, such as a cotton sports bra with a T–shaped back, and use elastic or a ribbon with no metal parts to tie back your hair.

## Before the Bout Begins

Before the weigh–in (which determines your weight competition category), a physician will check that you have no communicable diseases or skin infections. You should be clean shaven, unless you have had a beard for several months, and then it should be neatly trimmed. Short hair, or hair that is tied back is required, and your fingernails will be checked to be sure they are short.

For most events, after the weigh–in for international, regional and national competitive events, numbered lots are drawn at random to determine pairing. Each wrestler draws a number from a container, and then is paired with another number, e.g., Nos. 1 and 2 make a pair; Nos. 3 and 4 are the next pair.

## Officials

In general, three officials run the wrestling match: A mat chairman, a judge, and a referee. The mat chairman is the Supreme Court and settles any disagreement between the judge and the referee. The judge awards and records the points for each wrestler's actions, based on what the referee signals and his judgment of the action or holds. The mat chairman casts the deciding vote in any disagreement between the judge and referee. The referee is in charge of the bout itself and the two wrestlers on the mat. You'll notice that officials are dressed in white shirts, pants, and shoes. Additionally, the referee wears a red and a blue cuff; the red on his left arm, the blue on his right. If you are wearing a red singlet, the points you receive are indicated by the referee raising his left arm and signaling to the judge. When your name is called, go to the mat assigned to you. (The corner of the mat that is the same color as your singlet is where you stand.) The referee will be in the circle at the center of the mat and will call you and your opponent to his side, where he will examine both of you to see that you have no greasy cream or oil on your body and that you are not perspiring. He will check your hands and fingernails and determine that you have a handkerchief. The referee often uses a masculine French term, *Salut* (salute), to greet the two of you; you greet your opponent, shake hands with him, and start wrestling when the referee blows his whistle. The number of periods and the length of the bout vary for each age group and gender.

## The Bout and Scoring Points

The bout always begins from the Stance position—which you learned about in Chapter 3—and from then on, you earn points for successfully doing the following, either on offense (top position) or defense (underneath):

**Pinning** your opponent's shoulders to the mat for one–half of a second (differs for younger age groups) is what you want to achieve because that instantly makes you the victor. This move is also known as a

**fall**. A **technical fall** occurs when one wrestler has a 10–point margin in the bout.

Sometimes you win by a **decision**. This happens when you score more points than your opponent. An **injury default** can also end a match when an injury prevents your opponent from continuing.

A **takedown** is taking your opponent to the mat from the standing position.

A **reversal** is when your opponent frees himself from under you and takes control.

**Hand–to–hand** exposure is when you turn your opponent while he has his arms outstretched.

An **Escape** occurs when your opponent escapes from your control from the bottom position.

All of the above earn 1 point in international competitions.

A **High amplitude, or Grand, throw** occurs when a wrestler, from the standing position, causes his opponent to lose all contact with the ground, making his opponent describe a broad sweeping curve in the air, and brings his opponent to the ground in a direct and immediate danger position. (This throw is worth an additional 5 points, or 3 points if there is no danger.)

**Exposure** occurs when you are able to turn your opponent's shoulders to the mat. If you hold your opponent in this danger position for five seconds, you receive one extra point.

**Exposure, or Takedown then exposure,** is a combination maneuver and earns 2 points in international competitions.

If your match is tied at the end of the period, there is a three–minute, sudden death overtime (differs for younger age groups). Whoever scores first, wins. If neither of you score in the time allowed, the winner is determined by the officials.

In international wrestling, if neither one of you scored at least 3 points during regulation, there is a three–minute overtime (differs for younger age groups). Whoever gets 3 points first is the winner. If neither one of you does, the winner is determined by the officials.

Naturally, there are penalties when the rules are broken, as there are in any sport, and penalties earn points, but not the kind you want because your penalty points are awarded to your opponent.

An **illegal hold without consequence** will cost you 1 point, plus you are cautioned. A **caution** from the referee means an infraction of the rules has occurred.

An **illegal hold with consequence** is 2 points, plus a caution.

If you **flee the mat**, that's 1 or 2 points, plus a caution. A wrestler flees the mat when he is standing, or in the *par* (on the ground) position and is obviously avoiding his opponent.

If you **flee the hold**, that's 1 point, plus a caution. Fleeing the hold occurs when the wrestler obviously does not want his opponent to complete a hold.

Strictly forbidden and **illegal holds** are pulling hair, biting, pinching, pushing, strangling, or anything that appears to be torture or an attempt to physically hurt your opponent so you win through an injury default is forbidden. All these actions are self–defeating and illegal.

Because wrestling is an active sport, it is wise to learn it that way and perform it that way. Passivity is discouraged and means that you are not putting out enough physical effort by not initiating holds, or by holding your opponent with both hands to prevent him from wrestling, for example. If the referee sees passive activity, he will shout that player's color, e.g., Red! Red! Red! and issue a passivity warning. The referee can then give the more active wrestler the option of continuing the bout in either a standing or *par terre* position.

## When the Bout Ends

When the bout is over, shake hands with your opponent and wait for the official decision declaring the winner. Once the decision is announced, shake hands with the referee and your opponent's coach. These actions are important and risk a penalty if not observed by the participants involved. Finally, before you are allowed to wrestle in another bout, you must, in general, take a thirty–minute break.

Wrestling match officials have their own vocabulary of terms; although the French words are rarely used in domestic U.S. competitions. A partial list follows.

## International Officials' Vocabulary

**A Terre**—The bout is resumed in the "par terre" (literally, on the ground) position.

**Action**—The wrestler must execute the hold he has initiated.

**Attention**—The referee warns the passive wrestler before requesting a caution for refusal to assume the correct "par terre" position.

**Caution**—The penalty issued by the referee to a wrestler for violation of the rules.

**Centre**—The wrestlers must return to the center of the mat and continue the bout there.

**Contact**—The referee calls upon the wrestler to place both his hands on the back of his opponent, who is underneath. The wrestlers in the standing position must assume "body to body" contact.

**Continuer**—The bout must be resumed upon this order by the referee. The referee also uses this word to have the wrestling continued if the wrestlers stop due to confusion and look at him as if they are asking for an explanation.

**Danger**—The danger position.

**Dawal**—The referee encourages the wrestlers to wrestle more actively.

**Declare Battu**—The decision made subsequent to a defeat by obvious superiority.

**Defaite**—The opponent is beaten.

**Disqualification**—Disqualification is announced for unsportsmanlike conduct or brutality.

**Fault**—An illegal hold or violation of the technical rules.

**Fin**—The end of the bout.

**Gong**—The sound of the gong marks the beginning and end of a bout.

**Head Up**—The wrestler must raise his head. This order is given by the referee in the case of passivity and repeated attacks by a wrestler who thrusts his head forward.

**Jambe**—The wrestler has committed a leg error (Greco–Roman).

**Non**—This word is used to indicate that an action is not valid and is consequently void.

**OK**—The word most recognized internationally and means the hold is legal and correct.

**Open**—The wrestler must alter his position and adopt ̣ore open wrestling tactics.

**Out**—A hold applied outside the mat.

**Passif**—Passive red, passive blue. The warning given to the wrestler who is passive. It is signaled by raising the arm which bears the color of the wrestler at fault.

**Place**—By striking the mat with his hand and at the same time pronouncing the word "place," the referee reminds the wrestlers not to flee the mat.

**Salut**—The wrestlers must greet each other.

**Start**—The invitation to the wrestlers standing at opposite corners of the mat to step to the center to be examined and to shake hands. After this, they await the referee's whistle to begin wrestling.

**Stop**—This word means to stop the bout.

**Time out**—When one of the wrestlers stops wrestling, intentionally, or because of injury or any other reason, the referee uses this expression to ask the timekeeper to stop the clock.

**Touche**—The word used to indicate that the wrestler is beaten by a "fall." For a fall, the referee himself says "tombé," strikes the mat with his hand, and blows his whistle to indicate the end of the bout.

**Up**—The bout must be resumed in the standing position.

**Victory**—The referee declares the winner.

**Zone**—This word must be used and spoken in a loud voice if the wrestlers enter the passivity zone— the 1-meter wide band around the circumference of the mat.

## Other International Competitions

In addition to the Olympic Games every four years, there are several other international wrestling competitions that take place around the world in both Greco–Roman and Freestyle.

*Pan–American Games*

At Buenos Aires, Argentina in 1940, sixteen nations met to plan the first athletic contests for the nations of the Western Hemisphere, with their goal being to improve and increase understanding through amateur athletic contests. The first games, scheduled for 1942, were delayed by World War II so were not held until 1951 when 2,000 athletes from twenty countries competed in nineteen sports. By 1991, when the games were held at Havana, Cuba, they had expanded to include thirty–one sports, including wrestling and judo, which use the rules and regulations established by the FILA. Every four years, one year before the Olympic Games, this contest is held, and amateur athletes from the nations of North, South, and Central America, plus the Caribbean, compete. The games are conducted by the Pan–American Sports Organization, which consists of the Olympic Games committees from every participating country. The International Amateur Athletic Federation also cooperates in organizing and conducting the Pan–American Games.

*Asian Games*

Organization for the Asian Games began in India after World War II, with the purpose of developing intercultural understanding and friendship in Asia. An Olympic Council of Asia (OCA) coordinates these games with its forty-three member countries and regions. The first Asian Games were held at New Delhi in 1951, with eleven countries participating, and they are held every four years. The 1994 Games were in Hiroshima, Japan; the 1998 Games will be in Bangkok, Thailand. Whenever a country hosts the games, hours of time and effort are spent on official exhibits of architecture, art, music, painting, and sculpture in order to promote cultural exchange, along with the athletic contests themselves.

## World Cup

World Cup matches began in 1973 in Toledo, Ohio, with competition in freestyle wrestling only. By 1980, these games included Greco–Roman wrestling, but competitions in the latter style were usually held in foreign countries.

## World Championships

Beginning in 1961 at Yokohama, Japan, World Championships in wrestling have been held every year there are no Olympic Games. At the 1995 World Freestyle Wrestling Championship in Atlanta, Georgia, Kurt Angle was the first American to win a world title at 220 pounds. This 26–year–old from Pittsburgh, Pennsylvania entered the World Championships for the first time and won on his first try! Angle went on to win the gold at Atlanta in 1996 in the 100 kg. (220 lbs.) freestyle event.

## Goodwill Games

The Goodwill Games began in 1986 in Moscow and are held every four years in a Russian or American city. These games highlight the top individual wrestlers by weight class from nations around the world. So far, Americans have done well in these Games, with gold medal performances from John Smith, Bruce Baumgartner, Dave Schultz, Zeke Jones, Townsend Saunders, and others.

# 5

# USA WRESTLING

As wrestling grew into a popular national sport, it soon became obvious that America needed one group that would serve as the umbrella organization for wrestling in the United States, as FILA had done for international wrestling in Paris in 1912.

## USA Wrestling (USAW)

For many years, the Amateur Athletic Union governed wrestling in the United States, but during 1968 and 1969, the U.S. Wrestling Federation was organized and by 1975 had merged with the U.S. Kids Wrestling Federation. In 1983, the Federation became USAW and was recognized by both the U.S. and International Olympic Committees and FILA as the National Governing Body (NGB) for amateur wrestling in the United States.

Since 1969 when USAW held its first National Open Championships, the organization has grown to 135,000 members, with more than one-and-one-half million registered athletes since 1969, and has chartered more than 2,600 wrestling clubs. It continues with its original objectives: Graduates of high schools and colleges can enter competitive programs; officials, coaches, and wrestlers have opportunities to gain education and develop in

Greco–Roman and Freestyle wrestling; and wrestlers, coaches, officials and organizations that conduct wrestling programs have input regarding the policies and procedures that affect the sport of wrestling.

USAW works at the grassroots level to develop young wrestlers (both male and female), and trains and selects the teams that compete for the United States in national and international competitions. The group also organizes and runs regional and national championships for all wrestlers who are 9 years or older. There are camps, clinics, and educational programs for coaches, and USAW oversees the resident program for Greco–Roman and Freestyle wrestlers at the U.S. Olympic Training Center in Colorado Springs, Colorado. Here, amateur Greco–Roman and Freestyle wrestlers live, work, and train to improve their competitive skills.

## Divisions for Younger Wrestlers

The USAW has established wrestling programs at various age levels and has modified some of FILA's rules and applied them to different age and domestic competition categories.

At the scholastic level, USAW has set up age and weight categories for three Divisions—Kids, Cadets and Juniors. USAW uses modified FILA rules to accommodate these younger wrestlers who are eligible to participate at up to five levels of competition: local, regional, state, national and international, depending on age.

*Kids Division*

Schoolboy–Schoolgirl, Novice, Midget, and Bantam make up this division, each with its own weight and age categories. All members in this division are eligible to compete in local, regional, and state competitions, except those under nine years of age may not enter regional competitions. These young wrestlers are classed by age and weight, with age determined by birthdate. (For example, if your birthday is in the middle of the year, you are considered that age for the entire year.)

*Schoolboy–Schoolgirl (13-14 years old)*
This weight class begins at 70 pounds and increases in increments of 5 pounds to 175 pounds, with heavyweights weighing more than 175 pounds.

*Novice (11-12 years old)*
The novice category begins at 60 pounds and increases in increments of 5 pounds up to 165 pounds, with heavyweights weighing more than 165 pounds.

*Midget (9-10 years old)*
Midgets begin at 50 pounds, increase in increments of 5 pounds up to 130 pounds. Heavyweights weigh more than 130 pounds.

*Bantam (7-8 years old)*
The lightest weight class begins at 40 pounds and increases by five pounds for each class, with heavyweights weighing more than 75 pounds.

*Junior Division*
This division is for student–athletes who attended grades 9, 10, 11, or 12 during the school term a wrestling event was held. If the event was a summer tournament, then the athlete must have attended grades 9, 10, 11, or 12 during the school term just completed. The age requirement for the Junior Division is that you must not have reached your 19th birthday prior to September 1st of your senior year. Then, you have four consecutive calendar years of

eligibility, beginning with the ninth grade. Juniors are eligible for all domestic competitions in these twelve weight classes:

### Junior Division Weight Classes

| | | | |
|---|---|---|---|
| 1. Up to 98.0 lbs. | | 7. Up to 154.0 lbs. | |
| 2. Up to 105.5 lbs. | | 8. Up to 165.0 lbs. | |
| 3. Up to 114.5 lbs. | | 9. Up to 178.0 lbs. | |
| 4. Up to 123.0 lbs. | | 10. Up to 191.5 lbs. | |
| 5. Up to 132.0 lbs. | | 11. Up to 220.0 lbs. | |
| 6. Up to 143.0 lbs. | | 12. Up to 275.0 lbs. | |

*Cadet Division*

Cadets are 15–16 years and compete in domestic competitions in these thirteen weight classes:

### Cadet Division Weight Classes

| | |
|---|---|
| 1. Up to 83.5 lbs. | 8. Up to 143.0 lbs. |
| 2. Up to 88.0 lbs. | 9. Up to 154.0 lbs. |
| 3. Up to 94.5 lbs. | 10. Up to 167.0 lbs. |
| 4. Up to 103.5 lbs. | 11. Up to 182.5 lbs. |
| 5. Up to 112.0 lbs. | 12. Up to 209.0 lbs. |
| 6. Up to 121.0 lbs. | 13. Up to 242.0 lbs. |
| 7. Up to 132.0 lbs. | |

In Junior, Cadet and Kids competitions, protective headgear is recommended, and a face mask may be worn to protect an injury, if that is advised by a doctor. Some young wrestlers also wear knee pads and shin guards.

*University Division*

For wrestlers 18-24 years of age whose high school class has been graduated. The nine weight classes range from 110 lbs. to 286 lbs.

*FILA Junior World*

For wrestlers 17-20 years old. The ten weight classes range from 108 lbs. to 253.5 lbs. On the international level, this division is now called the Junior Division. The word Espoir is no longer used by FILA.

*Senior (Olympic) Division*

For wrestlers 19 years and older. The eight weight classes range from 119 lbs. to 286 lbs. Older wrestlers abide by FILA rules governing international competitions.

If you belong to a USAW chartered wrestling club, or are participating in a USAW sanctioned event at any level of competition, there are some modifications to FILA's rules that you, your parents, and your coaches should be aware of:

*Blood Rule*

1. Athletes known to be infected with the HIV/HBV virus cannot compete in any USA Wrestling sanctioned event.

2. Health care attendants known to be infected with AIDS cannot administer to bleeding athletes.

3. Anytime an athlete bleeds during a bout, the action shall be stopped immediately and first aid administered.

4. A bleeding athlete cannot compete unless the bleeding and spread of blood is effectively stopped. If the spread of blood to others cannot be effectively prevented to the satisfaction of the Chief Medical Officer and officials, then the athlete cannot compete further.

5. Time outs to stop bleeding or the spread of blood shall not be included in injury time. The cumulative time out to stop bleeding and the spread of blood shall not exceed five minutes.

6.  Blood must be cleaned from the mats, uniforms and bodies with a bleach solution, and all used towels and other cleanup materials must be properly and immediately disposed of in a separate container for contaminated material.

7.  Competition cannot resume until all blood has been removed and the cleaning solution residue has dried.

Other modifications have to do with weighing–in, pairing, drawing lots, and mat markings in national and international competitions. For additional information, ask your coach for details or consult a current rule book.

# SCHOLASTIC & COLLEGIATE WRESTLING

Although wrestling has been a competitive sport for centuries, its introduction into the standard curricula at the scholastic and college level in America occurred only in the 20th century when junior highs, high schools, and colleges included wrestling as a competitive sport in physical education classes.

## Junior High & High School Wrestling

Greco–Roman and freestyle are popular wrestling forms in America's junior high and high schools, but the most popular form is folkstyle. Folkstyle, also known as scholastic or collegiate wrestling, is a unique style practiced only in the United States. The folkstyle wrestler aims for control of his opponent while being fast and nimble on his feet, and legal holds are allowed both above and below the waist of your opponent.

The mat for scholastic competitions is no more than four inches thick and has a diameter of twenty-eight feet minimum, with a center circle area of ten–feet marked with parallel starting lines one–foot apart. The lines are one–inch wide by three–feet long and closed at the ends by a one–inch red or green line.

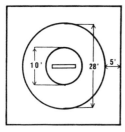

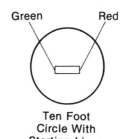

Green    Red

Ten Foot
Circle With
Starting Lines
National Federation of State High School Associations

**High School Wrestling Mats**

Your **singlet** will be in your school's colors and is cut higher on your torso and under the arms than those worn in national and international competitions. Full–length [but not Bermuda–length] tights are allowed. **Shoe** requirements are the same, non–slip **knee pads** may be worn, and protective **headgear** is required. If you are a member of the visiting team at a tournament, you will wear a red cuff on your left ankle when you are on the mat; the home team's wrestlers wear a green cuff.

Wrestlers are to report to the weigh–in clean shaven, with trimmed sideburns, and hair cut and under control. Your hair may not be braided, knotted or tied, but if it is, then you must wear a cover—a water–polo cap, for example—under your headgear. (If you have a beard, then a face mask is required.) However, a small, neatly trimmed mustache is acceptable. Body coloring, or marking (tatoos), and hair coloring are discouraged since they are distractions and can be offensive to others.

Thirteen odd– and even–numbered weight classifications are designated for scholastic competitions so no wrestler is overmatched.

| Junior High and High School Weight Classes | |
| --- | --- |
| 1. 103 lbs. | 8. 145 lbs. |
| 2. 112 lbs. | 9. 152 lbs. |
| 3. 119 lbs. | 10. 160 lbs. |
| 4. 125 lbs. | 11. 171 lbs. |
| 5. 130 lbs. | 12. 189 lbs. |
| 6. 135 lbs. | 13. 275 lbs. |
| 7. 140 lbs. | (a 215 lb. class is optional) |

After the weigh–in, a designated member of your team will participate in a coin or disc toss to determine which odd or even weight classification will begin the match. This toss also determines who chooses the starting position (up, down, or neutral) of the wrestlers for the second period of their bout. For the third period, the choice of positions is the reverse of how the wrestlers started the second period.

All wrestling matches have a common format, with a few variations: High school officials are dressed in black and white striped shirts, black trousers, black shoes, and wear green and red wristbands on their right and left wrists, respectively, to match the starting lines of the home and visiting teams. Three officials are involved—the referee, timekeeper, and scorer.

Before the bouts begin, the referee supervises the weigh–in, checks all the wrestlers to see that they are dressed properly, are well–groomed, and have no unhealthy skin conditions.

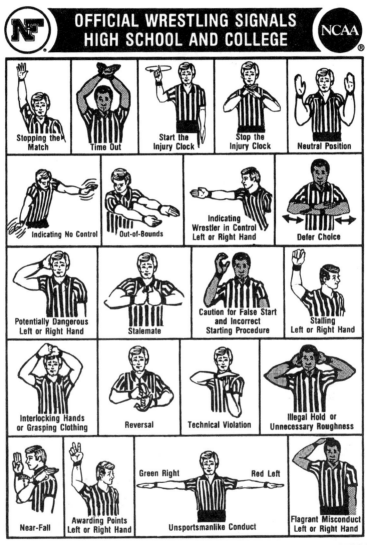

OFFICIAL WRESTLING SIGNALS
HIGH SCHOOL AND COLLEGE

Stopping the Match — Time Out — Start the Injury Clock — Stop the Injury Clock — Neutral Position

Indicating No Control — Out-of-Bounds — Indicating Wrestler in Control Left or Right Hand — Defer Choice

Potentially Dangerous Left or Right Hand — Stalemate — Caution for False Start and Incorrect Starting Procedure — Stalling Left or Right Hand

Interlocking Hands or Grasping Clothing — Reversal — Technical Violation — Illegal Hold or Unnecessary Roughness

Near-Fall — Awarding Points Left or Right Hand — Green Right / Red Left — Unsportsmanlike Conduct — Flagrant Misconduct Left or Right Hand

NCAA

A scholastic wrestling match lasts a total of 6–minutes—three 2–minute periods. There is a mandatory 45–minute rest break between bouts for each wrestler at tournaments. The first period begins with the opponents standing up and facing one another at their starting lines on the mat. The second period begins with one wrestler having a choice of top, bottom, or neutral (at least one foot on the starting line) position. Points are earned for how well holds and maneuvers are executed, and the match ends if one wrestler holds his opponent's shoulders to the mat for two seconds. If a **fall** is not achieved, a **decision** is made in favor of the wrestler with the most points. **Defaults** occur if one wrestler cannot continue the bout. A **forfeit** occurs when one wrestler does not show up for the match.

## How to Score Points
*Individual match points:*

| | |
|---|---|
| Near fall | 2 or 3 points |
| Takedown | 2 points |
| Reversal | 2 points |
| Escape | 1 point |

If the match is **tied** at the end of regulation (6 minutes), a 2–minute overtime period follows immediately, and the wrestler scoring the first points wins. A 30–second **tie breaker** takes place if no score is earned during the overtime period. One wrestler takes the top position with the opponent on the bottom. If the top wrestler scores or holds the bottom wrestler down, he wins. If the bottom wrestler scores, he wins. If there is still no score, the offensive, or more active and aggressive, wrestler is declared the winner.

Penalties and infractions of the rules follow the same pattern as those for national and international competitions. No potentially dangerous holds are allowed, as well as certain hammerlocks, headlocks, and strangleholds, to mention just a few of the illegal holds. Wrestlers will be penalized immediately for these infractions of the rules. Furthermore, stalling—avoiding contact, refusing to wrestle aggressively, delaying tactics—are penalized and not overlooked.

At the end of the bout, you remain on the mat with your opponent and shake hands with him, while the referee declares the winner. At no time during or after the bout should you be guilty of unsportsmanlike conduct, which includes throwing your headgear or lowering the shoulder straps of your singlet. Be aware that the referee knows the difference between "throwing" and "tossing" your headgear, and keeping your singlet straps up while on the mat is pretty obvious to everyone.

Information on the National Federation of Interscholastic Coaches Association (NFICA), the National Federation of Interscholastic Officials Association (NFIOA), and complete rules and regulations governing high school wrestling in the United States, contact the National Federation of State High School Associations at:

> National Federation of State High School Associations
> 11724 NW Plaza Circle, Box 20626
> Kansas City, Missouri 64195–0626
> Phone: (816) 464–5400

## Collegiate Wrestling

The first intercollegiate wrestling match took place in the United States when the University of Pennsylvania's team met Yale's in 1900. Wrestling's popularity spread so rapidly that within four years a wrestling conference was founded among some East Coast schools. However, it was the violence of college football that led to the formation of the National Collegiate Athletic Association (NCAA). Their response came, in part, from the violence of college football, especially the "flying wedge," which caused so many injuries and even deaths. The public's outcry that something had to be done to prevent violence from disrupting amateur athletics brought about a White House conference in 1905 to discuss what could be done to reform intercollegiate athletics. By 1910, the NCAA's Wrestling Rules Committee had in place a set of rules to regulate wrestling matches, and over the next twenty years, the NCAA began to issue standard rules and regulations for the sport and competitions. Today, they are the official governing body for amateur wrestling in U.S. secondary schools and at the college or university level.

Although several coaches solidified wrestling at the collegiate level in the U.S. during the first two decades of the 20th century, it was Edward Clark Gallagher at Oklahoma A. & M. (now Oklahoma State University) who made wrestling a varsity sport and built his teams into powerhouses. They suffered no defeats for ten years, from 1922–1931. Every four years many athletes competed at the Olympic Games, and collegiate wrestling was put on the map for the subsequent fifty years.

*Collegiate Wrestling Attire*

The one–piece wrestling **singlet** for collegiate competitions is cut higher in front and back and should not extend beyond the tops of your knees. You may wear full–length tights, but none that are Bermuda–length.

Your **shoes** should be heelless, above the ankle, and laced with eyelets. If you represent the home team, you'll wear a green cuff on your ankle; the visiting team wears a red cuff.

Protective **headgear** for your ears is mandatory, and it must lock in place so it won't come off or turn on your head, as this could cause an injury to your opponent. **Mouthguards** are recommended.

For reasons of health and safety, all wrestlers should be cleanshaven and well–groomed. Your hair should not grow below a standard shirt collar, sideburns and side hair should not grow below your ear lobes. A mustache is allowed, but it must be trimmed neatly and not hang down below your lower lip.

Usually, the referee supervises the weigh–in, and you will be examined by a doctor who will determine that you are not ill with any skin infections or communicable diseases. The NCAA has adopted standard precautions for the handling of blood–bourne pathogens (HBV and HIV), with some modifications that relate to athletic events. The most recent edition of the *NCAA Sports Medicine Handbook* can provide you with updated information.

The wrestling mat in collegiate wrestling has a wrestling area 32–42 feet in diameter, with a five foot apron around the wrestling area. Both these areas must be the same thickness, but no more than 4–inches. The wrestling area is marked on the mat by painted 2–inch wide lines. A circle 10–feet in diameter is painted at the center of the mat. Within this circle, are two 1–inch starting lines, 3–feet long and 10–inches apart. Two 1–inch lines close the ends of the starting lines. One of the two lines is green and is located closest to the home team, and the other is red and located closest to the visiting team.

In college folkstyle wrestling, competitors are separated into ten weight classes, ranging from 118 pounds to the heavyweight class of 177–275 pounds. The NCAA established a point system to keep score during a wrestling match, and this point total, plus the time of control, is used to determine a winner when there is no **fall**. For college wrestling, the match is divided into three periods also, but is 1–minute longer than a high school bout. The first period is 3–minutes; the second and third are 2–minutes each. In general, both high school and college wrestling focus on control, and points for **takedowns** and **reversals** are awarded, as are points for **controlling** an opponent. Any **illegal holds**, **stalling** tactics, and **fleeing the mat** are infractions of the rules and will draw penalties.

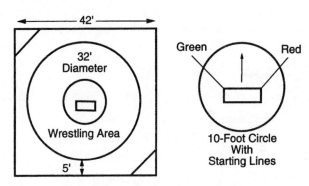

NCAA

**Collegiate Wrestling Mat**

*Individual Match Points*

| Takedown | 2 points |
|---|---|
| Escape | 1 point |
| Reversal | 2 points |
| Near Fall | 2 or 3 points |
| Riding Time Advantage 1 point, maximum | |

If the competitors are tied at the end of the three regulation periods, a 2–minute sudden death **overtime** is held. Whoever scores first, wins. If the score remains tied, there is a 30–second **tie breaker**, and whoever scores first, wins. If there is no scoring, the offensive wrestler is the winner.

## Summary of Rules

| Folkstyle | International |
|---|---|
| **Time:** | **Time:** |
| Three periods, 7 minutes (3-2-2) | One period, 5 minutes |
| **Fall:** | **Fall (Pin):** |
| Any part of both shoulders in contact with the mat for one second | Both shoulders held on mat |
| **Match Termination:** | **Technical Fall:** |
| 15–point advantage | 10–point margin |
| **Major Decision:** | |
| 8-14 points after 3 periods | |
| **Decision:** | **Decision:** |
| Fewer than 8 points after 3 periods | Wrestler scores more points in bout |
| **Overtime:** | **Overtime:** |
| If tied at end of regulation, a 2–min. sudden death overtime. Wrestler who scores first wins. | If neither scores at least 3 points in regulation, a 3–minute over-time period. If neither reaches 3 points, officials decide the winner. |
| **Tiebreaker:Tie Scores:** | |
| If no winner after 2-minute sudden death period, a 30–second tiebreaker. Whoever scores first, wins. If neither scores, the offensive wrestler wins. | 3–minute sudden death overtime. If tie not broken, officials decide the winner. |

As in high school wrestling, there is a similar end of bout procedure to follow, where the wrestlers wait for the decision from the scorer's table, the referee announces the decision, and the wrestlers shake hands. If the procedures are not observed by the contestants, an unsportsmanlike penalty is assessed. Behavior such as spitting, baiting your opponent, or throwing your headgear falls into this category and will result in a penalty being called against you and/or your team.

For more information on intercollegiate athletics, contact the NCAA at the address below:

National Collegiate Athletic Association
6201 College Blvd.
Overland Park, Kansas 66211-2422
(913) 339–1900

## Wrestling for Fun

If you belong to a wrestling club, there will be many opportunities for you to meet and compete with wrestlers from other clubs. These matches are pretty low–key and provide experience and fun without the pressures of formal competitions.

**Friendship Meets** take place when two or four clubs get together for a day–long event of three wrestling matches to practice techniques. These meets give you a chance to show your favorite hold. At friendship meets, there are no winners or losers, no awards are given, and there are no tournament costs.

**Ribbon Tournaments** are low–key with no weight classes, medals, or champions, and no one is eliminated if they lose. Wrestlers are grouped as nearly as possible by size, experience and ability, and everyone who participates receives a certificate. Lots get a certificate with a blue ribbon on it; losers get a red ribbon. The second round matches winners versus winners and losers versus losers of the first round. By the end of the day, nearly all participants have blue and red ribbons on their certificates, but the important thing is to have fun and make new friends; hence, the reason for the name of this tournament.

A **Technique Competition** shows how well you can execute different moves. Judging is based on your ability to execute different maneuvers. You'll need a partner for support while executing a move and will probably take on this supporting role yourself. There will be judges—at least three—sitting around the edge of the mat and awarding scores of 1–10 points to each wrestler. Each move is scored, and the wrestler with the highest point total for a certain move is champion of that move and receives a certificate or ribbon for his victory.

**Tournaments,** while real competitions, are still meant to be fun and are a chance to meet other young wrestlers from different areas. Often, medals, ribbons or trophies are given in every weight class.

There are many opportunities for wrestlers of all ages, weight, and skill levels to improve their skills and techniques to the point where they are able to compete on the national and international levels. A sport that usually begins as fun and "rough housing" as a kid can become a worthwhile challenge governed by the mental and physical self–discipline that can lead to long–lasting accomplishments. Get infor-mation on wrestling clubs in your area from:

USA Wrestling
6155 Lehman Drive
Colorado Springs, CO 80918
(719) 598–8181

# 7

# HEALTH & PHYSICAL FITNESS

You can't succeed in any sport without getting into and maintaining good health and physical fitness. A major fringe benefit of wrestling is that the fitness you develop while learning and training for that sport will carry over to any other sports or recreational activities you enjoy—soccer, gymnastics, swimming, or biking.

## Nutrition

Good eating habits go hand–in–hand with fitness training. An athlete can be in good health without being physically fit, but he can't get physically fit without following a well–balanced diet that contains protein, fats, and carbohydrates in the proper amounts. A proper nutritional program for Americans was summarized six years ago when the U.S. Department of Agriculture and the Department of Health and Human Services published detailed guidelines for a good diet. These guidelines emphasized the importance of carbohydrates and the lesser role of protein and fats in a healthful nutrition program.

Carbohydrates are sugars and starches and come in two forms—simple and complex. The simple form, found in processed foods like candy, soft drinks, or sweet deserts, is the one to avoid. These provide only "empty" calories that may taste good momentarily, but do nothing for overall health. It's not necessary to eliminate them entirely from your diet, but be selective. (Your dentist will be happy, too). Sugar, in its natural form, is abundant in fresh fruit, and a better way to satisfy a sweet-tooth is by eating a piece of fruit, rather than a candy bar. Complex carbohydrates are an athlete's best nutritional friend because they are his primary source of fuel. You'll find them in bread, vegetables of all colors (especially peas and beans), fruit, nuts, pasta, and whole–grains [(wheat, rice, corn, and oats.) They should make up about sixty percent of your daily food intake.

Protein is found in several foods—nuts, dairy products, and lean meats, poultry, and low–fat fish. But, a 16–ounce T–bone steak every day isn't needed to "build muscle." In fact, that's probably too much protein for your body to absorb efficiently; the rest just goes to waste. Try to keep your protein consumption to about twenty percent of what you eat each day, and you'll consume enough to build muscle, maintain it, and repair it when necessary.

Your body does need some fat, but not nearly as much as most Americans consume every day from a diet that is often overloaded with fat and salt. The fat you eat should come from margarine, vegetable oil, or nuts and should be no more than twenty percent of your daily intake of food. Fat has some benefits; it is an insulator in cold weather and an energy source, but a little goes a long way to keep an athlete healthy and fit.

Snacking in front of the television seems to be another American dietary habit, but for the athlete who is serious about wrestling and getting fit, there is no place for high fat, high salt, high calorie "junk food" in his diet. Try munching on an apple, tangerines, carrot or celery sticks while you watch your favorite show or when you need a snack during the day.

Don't skip meals—especially breakfast. Breakfast is like putting gas in your car—you need it to get started—and that meal should be a good, solid one-third of your daily calorie intake. Not hungry for breakfast in the morning? Try this once: Eat a light dinner the night before; you'll have an appetite in the morning, and that should help get you on a regular meal schedule. It is, perhaps, a cliche, but eating breakfast will make you feel better all day. Also, there is no nutritional law that requires a "traditional" breakfast. There is nothing wrong with eating a baked potato, having a hearty soup, or eating lean meat, fish, or poultry at your first meal of the day. The important point to learn is to eat well–balanced, nutritional meals throughout the day, starting with the first one.

A word on liquids: Avoid cola drinks, coffee, and tea. They are loaded with caffeine and act as diuretics to take water from your body. The one liquid you should not avoid is water, which is sixty percent of your body's weight and needed to lubricate your joints and maintain body temperature. Water is also the transportation system for the nutrients you need to stay healthy, so don't neglect this crucial liquid. One to two quarts per day will keep your body well–lubricated and prevent dehydration.

*Bulimia* and *anorexia nervosa* are two psychological and physical illnesses with their own forms of addictive behavior. Both young women and men have adopted these two damaging approaches to weight control. *Bulimics* try to diet, but then go on eating binges and follow–up by purging themselves with laxatives, vomiting, or by using diuretics. What begins innocently enough as an attempt to control weight can become an unstoppable habit requiring professional care.

*Anorexics* diet beyond just weight loss, and go to the extreme measure of starvation. If a person does not eat, his body takes energy from muscle tissue, including the heart. Such muscle damage can lead to heart failure and death. Like bulimics, anorexics need help from a professional. Karen Carpenter, a pop singer of the 1970s who had won three Grammys, and whose records had sold 30 million copies, died in 1983 of cardiac arrest brought on by years of being anorexic. She was only thirty–two.

Therapists agree that these two eating disorders stem from low self–esteem, a poor body image, and a desire to be perfect. The perfection, however, is often based on a beauty standard that is unattainable, i.e., trying to have the tall and thin body of a fashion model.

If you suspect you have an eating disorder, help is available from these groups:

National Association of Anorexia Nervosa and Associated Disorders (ANAD)
P.O. Box 7
Highland Park, IL 60035
(708) 831–3438

American Anorexia/Bulimia Association, Inc. (AABA)
418 East 76th St.
New York, NY 10021
(212) 734–1114

Overeaters Anonymous (OA)
4025 Spencer St., Suite 203
Torrance, CA 90504
(213) 542–8363

For youngsters, weight should not be controlled, but in older athletes, it can be managed in a healthy way. Coaches today place far more emphasis on weight management through a proper nutritional program. In fact, at the high school level, the rules require wrestling coaches to have a weight management program in place. This ensures that the wrestler will not lose strength or muscle, but will perform at the weight class that is right for his body type. High school wrestling programs require weight control programs, and your coaches will discuss body type and weight with you and decide in which age–weight category you belong. Try to maintain the weight level recommended by them and gain or lose weight according to their instructions. Follow their advice, and that of your parents, family doctor, or health care professional, about the diet and fitness training program that are best for you.

Finally, there are no "miracle foods" or "miracle diets" or "miracle pills" that will keep you in perfect health and physically fit. A well–balanced diet, paired with regular exercise, will help you stay in shape for life.

## Precautions

Approximately 40–50 million Americans smoke, and studies have shown that most of them began in their early teens. The use of cigarettes by teenagers is growing, and several steps are being proposed to limit sales to those younger than eighteen.

Based on recent statistical evidence from the Tobacco Intervention Network, young males seem most addicted to smokeless tobacco, wanting to imitate professional athletes, or succumbing to peer pressure.

Smokeless tobacco causes dental cavities—it is one-third sugar—and the irritation caused by holding a wad of tobacco in the mouth causes receding gums, gum disease, bone loss, and the inevitable tooth loss.

All drugs have side–effects, and smokeless tobacco is no different. It increases blood pressure, heart rate, and seems to increase the likelihood of kidney disease. Smokeless tobacco does not increase an athlete's reaction time. On the contrary, health, physical fitness, and a long life can be limited. Both the National Institute of Drug Abuse and the American Psychological Association agree that smokeless tobacco can produce dependency and result in addiction.

The use of any tobacco product by officials is not strictly prohibited, but is certainly recommended. Coaches, wrestlers, and team personnel at the high school level, however, are considered guilty of unsportsmanlike conduct if they use tobacco products.

In 1994, a national study found that smoking marijuana had doubled between 1992 and 1994 among teens. The Partnership for a Drug–Free America believes that there is an epidemic, yet many youngsters think smoking marijuana is not dangerous and is a "safe" alternative to alcohol or tobacco. With less marijuana smoking in the 1980s, young people have not seen "pothead burnout" among adults or their peers and are ignorant of the consequences.

The ramifications of smoking marijuana simply have not been publicized, but thirty years of research have pinpointed the effects of marijuana: According to Monika Guttman, who writes extensively about drug use, "marijuana reduces coordination; slows reflexes, interferes with the ability to measure distance, speed and time; and disrupts concentration, and short–term memory." (Everything on that list would be detrimental to any athlete, especially wrestlers.)

Marijuana has six times as many carcinogens [cancer causing agents] as tobacco, and today's marijuana is much more potent, creates dependency faster, and often becomes an "entrance" drug—one that can lead to dependence on "hard" drugs like cocaine.

Currently, nearly 12.5 million Americans use illegal drugs, and teenagers are the fastest growing portion of first–time, illegal drug users. The message American's need to hear is that drugs are illegal, dangerous, unhealthy, and wrong. Teens, especially, know that drugs are the most important problem they face—above violence, sex issues, and getting into college. Drug–prevention materials for young people and adults are available by calling the U.S. Department of Health and Human Services at this toll–free number:

1–800–729–6686

Steroids (anabolic–androgenic steroids, or AAS) are another drug danger, with terrible consequences for the user.

Steroid use by males can result in breast development, hair loss, acne, plus yellow skin and eyes. For females, breasts shrink, hair grows on the face and body, and menstrual cycles can become irregular. For both, the result of steroid use can be permanent stunting of body growth.

The psychological effects of steroid use are just as devastating, according to the American Sports Education Institute, which has noted the following: "Wide mood swings ranging from periods of violent, even homicidal, episodes known as 'roid rages' to depression, paranoid jealousy, extreme irritability, delusions, and impaired judgment."

The American Medical Association, the International Olympic Committee, the National Collegiate Athletic

Association, and the National Football League have deplored the use of steroids for muscle building or improving athletic performance.

## Vision and Dental Care

If you wear corrective lenses and want to wrestle, talk to your eye doctor and ask him if contact lenses would be suitable for you. Today's contacts come in hard and soft materials, are lightweight, and some can be worn for hours at a time. In fact, there are disposable contact lenses that can be worn twenty-four hours a day, don't need special cleaning, and can be disposed of after seven days. The latter are fairly expensive, however, and may not be suitable for the young, growing athlete. Always check with your doctor and get his recommendations for your unique needs. If you wear the traditional contacts, be sure to have your cleaning and wetting solutions with you at practices and competitions and let your coach know you wear contacts.

Wearing a mouthguard can prevent injury to your teeth, lips, cheeks, and gums, so use it at practices and competitions. Concussions or other head and neck injuries can be minimized by wearing a properly fitted mouthguard made by your dentist. It is not bulky, will not restrict your breathing, fits snugly, and covers your front teeth so well that you'll hardly know you're wearing it.

No matter what sport you play, custom mouthguards can help prevent oral injuries. They are especially important for young children just starting out in sports. In fact, if you get used to wearing one early, it will be easier to continue wearing one at the high school or collegiate levels where competition is far more aggressive.

## Physical Fitness and Conditioning

Just as the neophyte wrestler learns the seven basic skills, so too does he work on a conditioning program to build muscle, strength, and endurance, which can reduce the chance of an injury. Before you practice any of those seven basic skills, you need to do a short series of warm–up exercises. These will get your muscles warm and loose and make your heart beat faster, so you'll be ready for the falls and physical contact of wrestling practice.

A few good warm–ups are jogging, doing somersaults (both forward and backward), jumping, hopping, and with a partner, doing a wheelbarrow, and carrying your partner "piggy back." Next, loosen up with stretching exercises that help your flexibility, a major requirement in wrestling because flexibility can reduce your chances of a pulled muscle or injury. Stretching exercises should start from the top, at the neck, and work down to the legs, with arm, shoulder and lower back exercises in between. Do each exercise slowly and never stretch to a point that is painful. With a partner, or partners, you can do exercises that combine some wrestling moves, but naturally, you will do these exercises under the supervision of your coach.

The fireman's carry

A quarter–nelson

Hand control

Knee to chest

Two man pull–ups

Four man push–ups

Back arch

Back bridge hip heist

**Squats** are the leg strength building exercises you've probably done already with a partner when you've been practicing how to lift properly. They're repeated here as a reminder.

The **back arch** and **back bridge hip heist** are two exercises for the advanced wrestler and should only be attempted when your coach says you're ready.

Following a program of sensible eating habits, along with physical fitness and conditioning, can help to prevent setbacks in your wrestling program. The healthy, fit athlete is the one who will perform at his best and will truly enjoy the sport.

# 8

# Safety & First Aid

Wrestling is one of the safer sports for young athletes, but learning a few common safety rules can prevent serious injury. Since all athletes get bumps and bruises, and occasionally more serious injuries, here are a few precautions to take whenever you practice or compete:

## Safety First

- Always wear your headgear to practices and competitions. It's designed to protect your ears from injury and is recommended for all younger athletes. If your dentist has recommended a mouthguard, be sure to have it in your mouth during practices and competitions.

- Wear the right clothes for practice sessions. Don't wear "cut-off" pants with zippers or rivets or a belt with a metal buckle. They can scratch or gouge. Your gym shorts with a drawstring or elastic waist are best.

- Leave any jewelry in your locker or duffle bag. That includes watches, rings, earrings, etc. for boys and girls.

- Your coaches, or a designated helper, should make certain that there is extra room around the practice mats so you won't bump into furniture, walls, or other wrestlers. Occasionally, you might have to practice on mats that are not exactly the same as the ones used in tournaments. These should be put together with tape so they don't "slip and slide" during a practice or bout. This can prevent unnecessary injuries, even minor ones, and a vinyl mat cover can be useful as well in preventing some injuries.

- Pay attention to your teammates and point out anything hazardous they might be doing. It's easy to get hurt just "fooling around," so don't do this yourself and discourage your teammates from any activity that might cause an injury.

- Go through a warm–up session and do your stretching exercises before the actual practice or competition begins. This will prevent muscle strains and other aches and pains. If you're competing in a wrestling match that is interrupted for some reason, put on a robe or some kind of covering to keep warm. Cold muscles are more susceptible to injury, something you want to avoid.

- If you're not feeling well, skip a practice or two. You'll make a quicker recovery and be in better shape than if you practiced or competed while "under the weather."

- Drink plenty of water. Dehydration can happen quickly, so don't wait until you're thirsty to get a drink. Your coaches can recommend a sports drink, if they think they are useful, but water tastes just as good and is usually free, with no cans or bottles to dispose of.

## The First Aid Kit

Coaches know that eventually someone will probably sustain an injury of some kind. So it's wise to know what to do to handle those inevitable bumps, bruises, scrapes, or more serious injuries. Having a well–

stocked first aid kit handy is recommended. The basics in it should include the following:

- Adhesive tape in different sizes
- Adhesive bandages in different shapes and sizes
- Ammonia caps for dizziness
- Antiseptic solution for minor scrapes
- Antiseptic soap for washing a wound area
- Aspirin, or its equivalent, for simple headaches. For youth teams, no medication should be given without written, parental permission, signed and dated, authorizing the disbursement of aspirin, or any other medicine.
- Blanket to cover an injured player, since warmth reduces the chance of shock
- Cold packs
- Elastic wraps of various sizes
- Eyewash solution
- Gauze pads
- Hank's solution (trade name, Save–A–Tooth®) for a knocked–out tooth
- Plastic bottle filled with fresh water
- Sterile cotton sheets that can be cut to fit
- Scissors and, perhaps, an eyedropper and tweezers
- Tissues and pre–moistened towelettes
- Disposable towels and/or gauze pads
- A spray bottle or aerosol can containing chlorine bleach and water. A commercial disinfectant for cleaning blood from the mat may be used instead
- Antiseptic to clean blood from the wrestler
- Protective gloves
- Saliva boxes lined with disposable plastic bags.

Remember that Occupational Safety and Health Administration (OSHA) regulations must be followed when disposing of any items that have blood contamination.

It is a good idea to have a list of emergency telephone numbers taped inside the first aid kit, but in a real emergency, you can dial 911. Be sure you know where there's a telephone and have a few quarters in the first aid kit. At large tournaments, it is wise to have a physician, nurse, or other trained health care professional on hand to take care of serious injuries when they occur. But, never assume that precautions have been taken. Check in advance to be sure; be prepared.

Coaches may find these guidelines helpful:

- **Always Remain Calm.** Don't panic or appear flustered. Others around you will take their behavior cues from you.
- **Don't Try to be a Doctor.** When in doubt about the severity of any injury, send the player to his doctor or let the doctor, nurse, or health care professional on duty at the wrestling match make the decision.
- **Never Move a Player Who May Have a Serious Injury.** Don't try to make the wrestler more comfortable by moving him off the mat or into the locker room. This can make a serious injury worse. Be safe, not sorry, and call in the designated professionals if you have doubts about any injury. Under no circumstances should an unconscious wrestler be moved! Stay with him until the professionals arrive.

## Treatment

To treat the injuries that are fairly common in wrestling, the following guidelines are suggested:

*Scrapes and Mat Burns*

Wash scrapes and mat burns with an antiseptic cleaning solution and cover with sterile gauze. This is usually all that is needed to promote quick healing of these fairly common injuries.

*Muscle Pulls, Sprains, and Bruises*

Rest, ice, compression, and elevation **(RICE)** are the steps needed to handle these injuries and about all you should do in the way of treatment. Have the wrestler stop and Rest, apply Ice, Compress with an elastic bandage, and Elevate the injured arm, leg, knee, or ankle. Ice reduces swelling and pain and should be left on the injured area until it feels uncomfortable. Remove the ice pack and rest for fifteen minutes, then reapply. These are the immediate steps to take until the doctor arrives. **RICE** reduces the swelling of most injuries and speeds up recovery. Over the next few days, the injury should be treated with two to three twenty–minute sessions per day at two and a half hour intervals. This should provide noticeable improvement. Don't overdo the icing; twenty minutes is long enough. In most cases, after two or three days or when the swelling has stopped, heat can be applied in the form of warm–water soaks. Fifteen minutes of warm soaking, along with a gradual return to motion, will speed the healing process right along. But, seek the advice of a sports–medicine professional prior to starting your own treatment plan. Specially shaped pads are useful for knee and ankle injuries, and they can be used in combination with ice, compression and elevation. For a simple bruise, apply an ice pack.

*Head, Hand, and Foot Injuries*

Blows to the upper part of the head, especially near the eyes, can cause bleeding under the skin and the result is a black eye or eyes. An ice pack applied to the area will keep down the swelling until a doctor can look at the injury.

Normally, the eye can wash out most foreign particles with its ability to produce tears, but if this doesn't work, use eye cleaning solution to wash out the irritant. A few simple guidelines to follow are:

- Don't rub your eye or use anything dirty, like a cloth or finger, to remove the irritant.

- With clean hands, pull the eyelid forward and down, as you look down at the floor.

- Flush with eye wash, or use a clean, sterile cloth, to remove any particle you can see floating on your eye.

If the foreign object remains, tape a clean gauze pad over the eye and have the wrestler see a doctor.

Nosebleeds usually don't last very long, so have the wrestler sit quietly and apply a cold pack, while pinching the bleeding nostril at its base.

Communicable diseases, such as boils, "athlete's foot," ringworm, and "cold sores" may occur among wrestlers. Mouth sores may be treated with an "over–the–counter" medication, but check with your coach or doctor first before using any of these. The best medicine, however, is prevention, and you should avoid "skin–to–skin" contact with any wrestler who has any skin disorder.

A knocked–out tooth can be successfully replanted if it is stored and transported properly. The tooth should be placed in a transport container containing a solution such as Hank's or Viaspan®, which is available over–the–counter at a drug store.

The coach and all medical personnel at a wrestling event should be alert to the importance of how to care for a knocked out tooth. With immediate and proper attention to storage and transport, an injured wrestler may be able to have a knocked out tooth replanted successfully.

Jammed and/or broken fingers can be hard to distinguish, so use a cold pack to control swelling and pain. If there is no improvement within an hour, send the wrestler for an X–ray.

Small cuts need pressure to slow down bleeding. Then, wash with an antiseptic solution, cover with sterile gauze taped in place, and apply pressure. Of course, any deep or large cut might need stitches, so the wrestler should see a doctor as soon as possible.

Do not move a seriously injured wrestler, but get prompt medical attention or call for emergency aid. If you will have to wait for assistance, cover the injured wrestler with a lightweight blanket, since warmth will reduce the chance of shock. A wrestler who has a broken bone should be seen by a doctor. To safely move a person with an arm, wrist, hand, or leg injury, follow these steps:

- A finger with mild swelling can be gently taped to an adjacent finger.

- An elastic bandage may be gently wrapped around an injured wrist to give the wrist support. Do not wrap heavily and do not pull the bandage tight.

- If the wrestler has a possible broken leg or arm, the best approach is not to move the leg or arm in any manner. A cold pack can be used to lessen discomfort until medical personnel arrive, and the wrestler should be kept warm with a blanket or covering to avoid shock.

Blisters are fairly common problems for wrestlers and the best "medicine" is probably prevention. Well–fitting shoes and socks can go a long way toward preventing this annoying, painful injury. Any blisters that do occur should be kept clean and covered with a bandage, especially if the blister breaks. "Over–the–counter" medications to treat blisters are available, but follow your coach's or doctor's suggestions on these.

## Breathing and Heat Problems

Getting the wind "knocked out of you" is going to happen. Not much can be done to prevent this and not much can be done to treat this, but rest assured your breathing will return to normal more quickly if you can relax and take easy breaths.

Heat stroke and heat exhaustion do occur, but they can be minimized or avoided if wrestlers take plenty of water breaks. Coaches should monitor their wrestlers during practices and competitions to be sure the youngsters aren't getting dehydrated. If heat stroke or exhaustion do occur, have the wrestler lie down where it's cool and call an ambulance.

By following the guidelines in this chapter, the extent and severity of injuries can be reduced and treatment minimized so the player can return to the mat confidently. Knowing what to do is beneficial to players, coaches, and parents in and out of the sport.

# 9

## GUIDELINES

For everyone involved to get maximum enjoyment from a wrestling event, good sportsmanship must extend beyond the field of play—in wrestling's case, the mat—and include parents and spectators, as well as players and coaches.

### Hints for Parents and Spectators

Wrestling is meant to be fun for everyone involved, so parents need to be supportive, enthused about the sport, and keep it all in perspective by focusing on achievements, rather than miscues. Those attitudes will build the confidence a youngster needs to succeed, not just in wrestling, but in other activities as well. Parents, you are the earliest role models your children learn from and imitate, and they will carry over into sports the attitudes they have learned from you.

Parents want their kids to excel, to come out on top, and to be winners because they want to bask in their glory, even if it's only reflected. In wrestling, because it is an individual one–on–one sport, there is a winner and a loser. Parents must accept the fact that their child is going to lose sometime, so they need to be prepared to handle defeat in an adult manner by praising the effort involved and avoiding a litany of

"What you should have done was..." Most youngsters are pretty well aware of their skills, and they don't need to be told or made to feel somehow deficient when they lose. Likewise, parents should recognize the achievement of the victor and never criticize the officials or coaches.

Remember, coaches and officials are usually volunteers and are probably parents who have children involved in the sport. They have the same emotions you have—perhaps even more so, since they are more directly involved. But they have to be objective, treat all players with the same respect and regard, and follow the rules. You should, too.

Before attending a wrestling match as a spectator, learn a few basics about the sport, and your enjoyment will increase along with your understanding. Knowing some of the basic holds will help you follow the action on the mat. Wrestling is fast—most regulation bouts are three to five minutes—so plan to watch as many as possible to get a "feel" for the sport. Knowing how points are scored is also helpful because some matches will be decided on points scored, rather than a "pin" or a "fall." Observing a few common courtesies—sitting in your seat, not blocking anyone's view, not shouting at the officials, not criticizing the form or technique of a player, not arguing with other spectators—will make you a welcome spectator at any match. Any spectator who behaves in a manner that is considered unsportsmanlike conduct, will be asked to leave the match.

## Teams and Wrestlers

A truism of all sports is that learning to be a member of a team is one of life's crucial skills. Working together toward a goal rewards everyone involved with a sense of accomplishment, achievement, and pride in the effort. Win or lose, everyone learns from the experience.

Thumbs Up

**The team is ready for a match**

Mutual aid and dependability are needed from all members of a team, so be supportive of your teammates and let them know you can be depended upon to show up for practices and games. Also, there are a few specific things you can do for yourself and your team:

- Support each wrestler. Offer encouragement, especially in defeat, and congratulations in victory.
- Use positive, not negative, reinforcement. Point out the good holds and techniques.
- Let your coach correct errors. That's his job.
- Don't be a show–off.

- Try your best, go to every practice, and show that you are trying. Don't dwell on "mistakes,"—yours or anyone else's.
- Never be guilty of taunting—on or off the mat.
- Set a good example by staying healthy and physically fit.
- Remember, using tobacco products is considered unsportsmanlike conduct for players as well as coaches and team personnel.

As an individual wrestler, you need to keep the sport in perspective and fit it into your entire life, which means assigning priorities. You'll have to stay fit and healthy and get enough sleep each night. Since many schools require that a certain level of academic achievement be maintained in order to participate in sports, school attendance and school work cannot be neglected in favor of concentrating on athletics. For you, wrestling can be a rewarding experience, if you remember the following:

- Compete because you want to. Don't let someone "pressure" you into wrestling.
- Obey the rules.
- Don't argue, whine, or gripe about calls or decisions.
- Keep your temper in hand and never retaliate.
- Prepare, do your best, and have fun.
- Finally, the Golden Rule does work. Treat everyone the way you want to be treated.

Being a dependable member of your team, learning from your coaches, following their guidelines, and playing fair with opponents can make your wrestling experience a life–long guide to achieving other goals.

Wrestlers should behave in such a way that they are a credit to their schools, the sport and themselves. The image of the sport depends on your behavior and appearance, not only at matches, but also while traveling, and at school or away. Your conduct can influence your teammates as well as whether or not you win or lose.

Thumbs Up

Spectators

## Coaches

Just as parents are the first "real life" role models for children, teachers and coaches come next. Coaches have immediate and quite visible responsibilities to their charges so set the example you want them to follow. Be on time for practices, keep yourself fit and healthy, praise and criticize positively. Kids develop an intuitive alarm that goes off when someone breaks the rules. Be fair, and never use your position of authority to gain an unfair advantage for yourself or your wrestlers.

The use of tobacco products by coaches draws an unsportsmanlike conduct penalty in scholastic wrestling, so it is important to know the rules and enforce them uniformly, not only with the wrestlers but also all team personnel. Taunting others is expressly prohibited and can result in the coach, his wrestlers, the team, and other personnel being hit with an unsportsmanlike conduct penalty.

The ethical obligations of coaches are broad and deep and extend beyond practices and competitions to include other members of the academic and non-academic wrestling communities. Building character, integrity, respect, and assuring the physical well-being of your wrestlers are integral parts of your coaching duties and should be included in the total learning experience of young wrestlers.

# 10

# WRESTLING WRAP-UP

## The Benefits of Wrestling

Wrestling is an equal opportunity sport—it's for every kid—short or tall, chubby or skinny. Because of its age and weight category system, kids are never over–matched, which could be demoralizing or intimidating. This is a sport where everyone participates since there are no "bench warmers" or "subs" or "designated hitters." Wrestling has a soft impact on the pocketbook, too, for no large investment in bats, balls, gloves, rackets, expensive lessons, or fancy gear is required. Many sports demand hours of training and practice to learn how to shoot baskets or hit or kick a ball. Not wrestling.

Wrestling is a "natural" activity that most youngsters seem to engage in at some time or another—on the floor in the family room, or outside in the yard. To channel this youthful energy, there is no better sport than wrestling. As a year round activity, wrestling doesn't need a "season," which prevents the ups and downs of getting in shape. Wrestling teaches lifetime good health and physical fitness, while the coordination, agility, and flexibility learned in wrestling can be used to advantage in other sports. Wrestlers learn teamwork, good sportsmanship, fair play, and the ability to get along with others in a competitive setting, while relying on the individual's skills. The sport involves entire families at many levels of competition, from elementary school through college and beyond. Besides, wrestlers make great role models. Many attend college and get their degrees in a range of academic disciplines from bacteriology, business, and education to genetics, history, and psychology.

Physically, wrestling builds muscles, flexibility, and strength. It teaches lifetime good eating habits and warns of the health hazards of alcohol, tobacco, and drugs. Mentally, this one–on–one sport builds self–confidence and a "can–do" attitude. Wrestlers learn to set goals and to achieve them. In this mental action/reaction sport, the wrestler must concentrate and think against one opponent. Wrestling teaches self–control and independence and instills the discipline needed to say no to temporary pleasures in favor of long–range rewards. Socially, a wrestler develops respect and admiration for others and their abilities. He learns to obey and play by the rules and to accept the decisions of adults. The wrestler gains valuable experience in teamwork, cooperation, and the need to subordinate his own wishes to that of an overall team effort.

## Athletes with Special Needs – USABA

In 1976, the United States Association of Blind Athletes (USABA) was founded as a nonprofit member of the U.S. Olympic Committee to train blind and visually impaired athletes for national and international competition. Its more than 3,000 members compete in nine sports: alpine and nordic skiing, goalball, judo, powerlifting, swimming, tandem cycling, track and field, and wrestling.

USABA's major goal is to assure that legally blind athletes get the same competitive opportunities as other sighted athletes.

At the 1994 Winter Paralympic Games in Lillehammer, Norway, athletes from USABA earned five medals—the highest count for blind athletes in the history of the Winter Games. Wrestling Nationals for USABA members were held in Indianapolis, Indiana, on March 29 and 30, 1996.

Additionally, USABA hosts more than 400 events every year for blind athletes, who have been able to train at the Olympic Training Centers in Colorado Springs, Colorado, and at Lake Placid, New York. The group is headquartered at the Colorado School for the Deaf and Blind in Colorado Springs, Colorado, and further information may be obtained by writing or calling them at the address below:

USABA
33 N. Institute St.
Colorado Springs, CO 80903
(719) 630–0422

## Volunteering

Being a volunteer requires some extra time and a desire to make a difference in the lives of young people. Wrestling is a golden opportunity for everyone in a family or the community at large to get involved and make this difference. Today more than ever, young people need to know adults care about them and their futures, since they are bombarded, literally, everyday by enticements to use drugs, join gangs, or engage in other activities that promote a dangerous lifestyle.

There are many ways you can help your local wrestling club, as a coach or leader, official or fan.

When a local club or school is sponsoring a tournament, you could volunteer to help in a number of ways:

- Help set up the area where competitions will take place.
- Man the on–site registration table.
- Conduct the weigh–in or be a pairing chief.
- Be a timer, scorer, or runner.
- Be the announcer.
- Be the tournament coordinator.

## Coaching

USAW has a four–level coach certification program—Copper, Bronze, Silver, and Gold—for its more than 10,000 active coaches, and USAW oversees the 2,000 officials who belong to the U.S. Wrestling Officials Association (USWOA). Educational programs for coaches are offered covering a range of topics from psychology to strength training, to diets for combating fatigue, along with explanations of the rules for coaches and wrestlers. Technique clinics are held to demonstrate offense and defense so that wrestlers and coaches may improve their skills.

## Organizations for Coaches and Officials

The National Wrestling Coaches Association (NWCA) includes members from both the collegiate and scholastic levels who meet regularly and network extensively.

The National Federation of Interscholastic Coaches Association (NFICA), and the National Federation of Interscholastic Officials Association (NFIOA) are the national groups for coaches and officials at the high school level. More information on these two groups can be obtained by contacting the National Federation.

National Federation of State High School Associations
11724 Plaza Circle (P.O. Box 20626)
Kansas City, MO 64195–0626
(816) 464–5400

## National Wrestling Hall of Fame & Museum

A national museum for wrestling was the idea of Myron Roderick, the first executive director of USA Wrestling, and Dr. Melvin D. Jones, an insurance executive and avid wrestling fan. Funded by popular subscription, the museum was dedicated in 1976. Located near the campus of Oklahoma State University in Stillwater, Oklahoma, the National Wrestling Hall of Fame and Museum commemorates and celebrates the sport of wrestling in America. The Hall has three major areas and themes.

Great athletes, coaches and contributors are spotlighted in the Honors Court. A Wall of Champions lists the names of 4,500 American wrestlers who have starred in national and international competitions. And, the library contains an expanding collection of materials on wrestling— books, films, and videos.

Finally, the Hall of Fame promotes wrestling nationwide and focuses on family participation so that parents are involved along with their children.

The classic green marble sculpture, *The Wrestlers*, that graces the lobby of the Museum and weighs more than three–quarters of a ton, is a copy of the original housed at the Uffizi Gallery in Florence, Italy.

For more information, contact the Hall of Fame at the address below:

National Wrestling Hall of Fame and Museum
405 W. Hall of Fame Ave.
Stillwater, OK 74075
(405) 377-5243 (405) 377-5244 (Fax)

# GLOSSARY

Wrestling has its own vocabulary of terms and definitions unique to the sport, and a separate vocabulary for officials. (See Chapter 4, "The Wrestling Match"). Learning most of these will increase your knowledge of the sport and add to your enjoyment, whether you are competitor or spectator.

## General Terms and Definitions

**Age**—A wrestler's age is the birthday he has during the calendar year. For example, if he becomes 15 in July, 1996, he is considered 15 all year.

**Amplitude**—A throw when the opponent is lifted above the thrower's waist. Points differ for high and low amplitude throws.

**Blind draw**—Drawing of lots. All positions are determined by chance. There is no seeding or separation.

**Blue pool**—The wrestlers with even draw numbers.

**Body lock**—When you lock your hands around your opponent's body to execute a throw.

**Bout**—The competition between two wrestlers; a match.

**Bridge**—When a wrestler supports himself on his head, elbows and feet to keep his shoulders from touching the mat.

**Brutality**—Unnecessary roughness. The motive is to injure your opponent. Penalty is disqualification from the tournament.

**Cadet**—The 15–16 age group for wrestlers.

**Call to the mat**—Two wrestlers are called to report to a specific mat for their competition.

**Category**—The age group in which a wrestler competes.

**Caution**—The penalty against a wrestler for an illegal hold, fleeing a hold, fleeting the mat, or refusing to take a starting position in *par terre*.

**Center**—Starting area in the center of the mat. Also, an instruction to the wrestlers to return to the center.

**Central wrestling area**—The middle of the mat, 7 meters across (in national and international competitions), where the action should take place.

**Correct hold**—A well–executed throw. Not a takedown, or putting the opponent in danger. A point may be awarded for "appreciation" of the throw.

**Counter**—A defensive action that stops or blocks the offensive wrestler's attack. Points can be awarded for a counter.

**Decision**—Victory on points. The margin can be from 1 to 9 points in international matches.

**Default**—A bout ends in default when one wrestler is injured and can't compete.

**Disqualification**—One or both wrestlers are eliminated from a bout.

**Division**—Age group or category in which a wrestler competes. (See Category.)

**DNWI**—Notation that a wrestler did not weigh–in.

**Draw number**—Number drawn by lot to identify each wrestler.

**Drawing of lots**—The time when random selection of numbers by each wrestler at the weigh–in takes place.

**Drug testing**—Ordered for any contestant at any time, at any national or international event or trials, at the request of FILA, the U.S. Olympic Committee or USA Wrestling.

**Elimination**—Removal of a wrestler from the competition. A second defeat, an injury, forfeit, failure to weigh in, or misconduct can result in elimination.

**FILA Junior World**—The 17–20 age group. (Wrestlers 16 years of age may enter this division with a medical certificate.)

**Escape**—Wrestler gets out from under opponent, gets on his feet, and faces his opponent.

**Exposure**—Occurs when the defensive wrestler's back is turned toward the mat. The head or an elbow are not touching the mat. Earns one point.

**Face mask**—A protective cushion worn due to an injury. Allowed by USA Wrestling if prescribed by a doctor or by the chief medical officer of the event. Forbidden in international events.

**Fall**—Victory by pinning an opponent's shoulders to the mat.

**FILA**—Fédération Internationale des Luttes Associées. The international governing body of wrestling.

**Fleeing a hold**—Refusing contact to prevent your opponent from initiating or executing a hold. Punished with a caution, a penalty point, and choice of position to your opponent.

**Fleeing the mat**—Leaving the wrestling area. Avoiding your opponent's attack. Punished with a caution, a penalty point, and choice of position to your opponent. Two penalty points if fleeing occurs from a danger position.

**Freestyle**—One of the two international wrestling styles. Use of the legs is permitted.

**Folkstyle**—The wrestling style at U.S. schools and colleges. Very active with holds allowed above and below the waist.

**Grand Amplitude hold**—A high, sweeping throw when you lift your opponent completely off the mat.

**Greco-Roman**—One of the two international styles. Attacking your opponent's legs, or using your own legs in an attack, is prohibited.

**Gut wrench**—A hold using the defensive man's torso and turning him to score points.

**Handkerchief**—Each wrestler must have one, and must show it to the referee when he gets to the mat.

**Headgear**—Ear protectors. Recommended by USA Wrestling at the Junior and younger levels. Optional for Espoirs and Seniors, if the opponent does not object. Forbidden in international events.

**Illegal hold**—A hold or maneuver forbidden by the rules. Punishment is a caution and one or two penalty points.

**Injury time**—Bout interrupted because a wrestler is hurt. Two minutes total allowed each contestant in one bout.

**International styles**—Freestyle and Greco–Roman.

**Instantaneous fall**—The simultaneous touch of both shoulders by either wrestler. Not a fall. Two points for the opponent.

**Judge**—One of the officials, seated across from the mat chairman and timer. The judge assists the referee, awards points and keeps score.

**Junior**—Nationally, a high school wrestler attending grades 9, 10, 11, or 12 during the school term of the event (or immediately before a summer event), and less than 19-years-old on September 1 of the year of the event.

**Jury**—The referee, judge, and mat chairman. The officiating team.

**Jury of Appeal**—The protest committee.

**Kids**—The USA Wrestling division for wrestlers 14 and younger.

**Mandatory rest**—A wrestler must have at least 30 minutes after a bout before he can compete again. For high school bouts, the rest must be 45–minutes.

**Mat chairman**—Chief of the three–man officiating team. He decides on the score or action if the referee and judge disagree.

**Medical certificate**—Written statement from a physician that a contestant is capable of competing.

**Medical examination**—A doctor checks each wrestler for skin infections or contagious disease right before the first weigh–in.

**Medical officer**—A physician, trainer or other medical professional who treats injuries suffered by the contestants.

**Modifications**—Variations in the FILA rules adopted by USA Wrestling for domestic competition and applied to specific age groups.

**National Collegiate Athletic Association (NCAA)**—the official governing body for college and university wrestling in the United States.

**National Federation**—USA Wrestling, the national governing body for wrestling in the United States.

**Olympic division**—The 19–and–over age group. Wrestlers 17–18 may enter with a medical certificate. Also called Open or Senior division.

**On deck**—Two wrestlers waiting their turn for the next bout on the same mat.

**Outstanding wrestler**—The most skilled competitor in an event receives this award.

**Overtime**—Occurs when the leading wrestler has not scored three technical points, or the score is tied at the end of the regulation bout.

**Paddles**—Red, white and blue scoring devices, similar to table tennis paddles, used by the judge and mat chairman to indicate their decisions.

*Par terre*—When both contestants are wrestling down on the mat, literally "on the ground."

**Passivity**—Stalling and avoiding combat. Penalized by warnings and the passive wrestler is placed underneath in the *par terre* position.

**Passivity zone**—1–meter wide band inside the edge of the mat. When the referee shouts "Zone!" the wrestlers must work toward the center of the mat.

**Pool**—Group.

**Protection area**—Out–of–bounds area of the mat.

**Protest**—A formal appeal to reverse a decision, claiming an error.

**Referee**—The official who runs the bout on the mat. Starts and stops action. Signals his decisions on points, position and passivity to the judge and mat chairman.

**Reversal**—When the wrestler underneath reverses his position and comes to the top position in control. One point value.

**RICE**—Acronym for Rest, Ice, Compression and Elevation. The suggested formula for immediate management of an injury.

**Risk**—The concept that a wrestler cannot succeed without taking chances. Refusing to take risks is passivity.

**Round**—A series of bouts involving all the wrestlers in a weight class or group, once each.

**Scoreboard**—Unofficial way to show the score of a bout to the spectators.

**Seeding**—Pre–tournament ranking of contestants by past achievement. Separates them in the draw.

**Senior**—Another name for the Olympic or Open division, ages 19 and up.

**Singlet**—The one–piece uniform worn by the wrestler. Red singlets are worn by odd numbers; blue by even numbers drawn.

**Singlet colors**—For each bout, one wrestler wears a red singlet, the other a blue singlet. In high school and college, singlets are in school colors.

**Slam**—Throwing an opponent down with unnecessary force and not going to the mat with him. May be considered brutality. Illegal throw in Kids competition.

**Takedown**—Wrestler takes his opponent to the mat from a standing position. Earns one point.

**Team leader**—The person who leads a delegation on an international tour.

**Team scoring**—The ranking of clubs, states or other teams determined by points awarded for the success of their wrestlers.

**Technical fall**—A slang term for victory by technical superiority.

**Technical points**—Points scored by the wrestlers for actions and holds during a bout. Penalty points are technical points.

**Technical superiority**—A victory by a margin of 10 or more points.

**Tombé**—French word for fall. The referee says this word to "count" the time for a fall, about one-half second.

**Total wrestling**—The concept that both wrestlers must give maximum effort at all times. (See Risk).

**Universal wrestling**—Use of a wide variety of techniques and holds.

**University**—USA Wrestling division for wrestlers ages 18–24 and whose class has graduated from high school.

United States Association of Blind Athletes (USABA)—The national association of blind athletes in the United States.

USA Wrestling—The national governing body for wrestling in the United States. The delegate to the U.S. Olympic Committee and to FILA.

Weigh–in—Before a competition, when a wrestler steps on the scale to certify that his weight is not above the limit for the class in which he is entered.

Weight classes—Grouping by size for competitions. Divisions are in pounds or kilograms.

World Cup—A dual meet competition that is held annually with teams from different continents.

Zone—Word used and spoken in a loud voice if the wrestlers enter the passivity zone.

## International Terms

| USA Wrestling | FILA |
| --- | --- |
| Announcer | Speaker |
| Caution | Warning or Caution |
| Warning | Passivity |
| Chief pairing master | Secretariat |
| Disqualification (cautions) | Disqualification |
| Disqualification (misconduct) | Brutality |
| Olympic, Open or Senior Div. | Senior division |
| Overtime | Extension |
| Paddles | Bats |
| Pools | Groups |
| Protest committee | Jury of appeal |
| Round–robin | Group finals |
| Scratch weight | No tolerance |
| Start sheet | Programme |
| Technical fall | Technical superiority |
| Weight allowance | Tolerance |

T.M.

# USA**wrestling**

USA Wrestling is the National Governing Body for the Sport of Wrestling in the United States and, as such, is its representative to the United States Olympic Committee. Simply, USA Wrestling is the central organization that coordinates amateur wrestling programs in the nation and works to create interest and participation in these programs.

It is not the wild or "off the top rope" wrestling world you might have seen on television. The many programs and activities conducted by USA Wrestling, or by the hundreds of chartered clubs, provide opportunities for youth and adults alike to gain an understanding an appreciation for the international styles of wrestling. These encompass Freestyle and Greco-Roman wrestling, as well as folkstyle (scholastic and collegiate), which is the style practiced at high schools and colleges across the country.

USA Wrestling has more than 135,000 members, including athletes of all ages, coaches, officials, parents and fans striving together to strengthen the sport. Part of USA Wrestling's mission is to foster grassroots development for the sport.

Each year, USA Wrestling charters more than 2,600 wrestling clubs and sanctions more than 1,500 local, state, regional and national competitions. These opportunities and more are just a small part of the exciting world of wrestling.

*Your purchase of items available through USA Wrestling helps support the organization at all levels.*

*Wrestling equipment, apparel and educational materials, including wrestling shoes, shirts, earguards, singlets, kneepads and an extensive selection of wrestling souvenirs, as well as training videos and books*

*may be purchased by contacting:*

**USA Wrestling**
**6155 Lehman Drive**
**Colorado Springs, CO 80918**
**(719) 598-8181**
or
**by visiting us at our Web site:**
**http://www.usawrestling.org/**

# United States Olympic Committee
## Sports Series Order Form

(Please print):

Date:_____

Name: _____

Address: _____

City:_____State:____Zip: ____

Phone:(___) _____

| Title | Price | Qty / Amount |
|---|---|---|
| *A Basic Guide to Archery* | $7.95 | ____/_____ |
| *A Basic Guide to Badminton* | *$7.95* | ____/_____ |
| *A Basic Guide to Cycling* | $7.95 | ____/_____ |
| *A Basic Guide to Decathlon* | $8.95 | ____/_____ |
| *A Basic Guide to Equestrian* | $7.95 | ____/_____ |
| *A Basic Guide to Soccer* | $7.95 | ____/_____ |
| *A Basic Guide to Wrestling* | $7.95 | ____/_____ |
| *Olympism* | $8.95 | ____/_____ |

Subtotal: _____

8.25% tax (CA only): _____

**S/H charges:**
1 title                $2.50
each additional title  $1.00

S/H: _____

Total: _____

Send this order form with payment (check, money order or credit card info), to the address at the right.

**Griffin Publishing**
544 W. Colorado Street
Glendale, CA 91204

Credit cards: VISA or MasterCard only.
(circle one) **VISA   MC**

Account number _____

Expiration date ___/___

Signature _____

For faster service on credit card orders call 1-818-244-1470 or Fax  1-818-244-7408.